AF522398

LIVING A LIFE

LIVING A LIFE

RAVI SAWHNEY

Konark Publishers Pvt. Ltd

New Delhi

Konark Publishers Pvt. Ltd
206, First Floor,
Peacock Lane, Shahpur Jat,
New Delhi 110 049
+91-11-41055065
india@konarkpublishers.com, us@konarkpublishers.com
www.konarkpublishers.com

First Impression 2023

The photographs used in this book are from the author's collection.

ISBN: 978-81-956786-3-1
Edited by Padma Alva
Cover Design by Misha Oberoi
Printed and bound at Saurabh Printers Pvt. Ltd.

Dedicated to

My parents ***Madan Mohan*** *and* ***Krishna Sawhney***
for giving me a great start to life;
My wife ***Madhu****, my daughters* ***Ravina****,* ***Aushima*** *and* ***Raisa****,*
and to my grandchildren ***Riana*** *and* ***Aryan***
who have inspired and enriched my life with
their love and commitment

Contents

Pre-Publication Reviews

Memoirs can mimic fiction, borrow style from tabloids, substance (or the lack of it) from the open library of gossip. They can entertain, divert, help pass a journey more congenially. They can also bore you out of your wits. And make you hate yourself for having even tried to read the stuff. But this book is different.

Ravi Sawhney tells his life's story not because he thinks it is unique, instructive or will change the reader's idea of life. He tells it because he has a story to tell that rings true, as true as a chiming bell atop a monastery. Reading it has been an utter delight. It is as frank as frank can be but not one person, not one institution, has her or his name introduced to the dust of ridicule or the mist of flattery. It has taste. It has truth.

—Gopalkrishna Gandhi
Former Administrator, Diplomat and Governor

Simply written and easy to read, this volume narrates the exciting experiences and notable achievements of a young man who gave up a glorious future as an upcoming national athlete to become a minion of the state—an IAS officer who earned high distinction while serving the Punjab and the Union Governments, and enviable recognition during his two decades-long scintillating tenure as an international civil servant.

The author can proudly look back and rejoice over the evolution of his career—from mobilizing village leaders to set up a cooperative milk plant in Punjab to advising the Presidents of the new Central Asian Republics about the gains of pursuing sound economic approaches in their nation building tasks. As a pivotal functionary in ESCAP, the author was responsible for structuring BIMSTEC and SPECA and establishing NIST, a school of international standards in Bangkok, where he presently lives and continues to drink Life to the lees. The book is inspirational and highly recommended for educational institutions and training academies.

—**N.N. Vohra**
Former Governor Jammu & Kashmir

Compliments to Ravi Sawhney. This is one of the best memoirs I have read—an excellent exposition of the role of an IAS officer in providing good governance and the challenges faced in getting positive results despite outmoded rules and regulations, roadblocks at different levels, dealing with politicians with their own agenda and egos, and above all mounting expectations. With tireless effort, initiative and foresight he adjusted to tasks from rural development, to setting up a milk plant, to industrial development, to handling political turmoil in Punjab, and to dealing with a variety of jobs not only at state and national level but taking on responsibilities with an UN organisation as well. Above all what gave him the most satisfaction was the difference he was able to make to the lives of people.

In his own words, 'And when I was back at my work sitting amidst the rural poor and the deprived, I could feel how much they depended on me to help them in meeting their basic needs and to make their lives more dignified—it was a matter of great satisfaction that one was actually making a difference in improving their lives.' Vignettes from his personal life add to the interest. A compulsory reading, particularly for aspirants and fresh entrants to the service.

—S.K. MISRA
Former Principal Secretary to Prime Minister

Here is a very readable book by a retired IAS officer about a working life that involved promoting agricultural development, bringing in new industries to generate employment, resolving local conflicts that could have become violent, attempting to prevent a major political setback, becoming a manager of a trade promotion initiative of the Union Government and going on to working in an international organisation for promoting cooperation in Asia. This is the life of an IAS officer that should tell many people, including the young who are contemplating working for the government, how challenging and fulfilling that life can be.

—NITIN DESAI
Former Under-Secretary-General for Economic & Social Affairs, United Nations

Preface

I belong to a generation born when the situation in the world was tumultuous. The Second World War was still raging in Europe, but the tide was beginning to turn in favour of the Allied Forces. Near home, the Indian troops under the British command were fighting to evict the Japanese Army from Burma (now Myanmar). Within our country, Mahatma Gandhi's call for 'Quit India' in 1942—demanding an end to the British rule in India—had evoked strong and retaliatory action from the British government, culminating in the imprisonment of Gandhi and all frontline leaders of the freedom movement and leading to the outbreak of violence in various parts of the country.

Our family lived in the North-West Frontier Province and was involved in trading, forest contracts and sugar industry. I was born in Abbottabad, a cantonment town in the Khyber foothills of the North-West Frontier Province. We moved across to Punjab a year before the Partition of India, as my father, anticipating that the sugar mill in Mardan would become part of Pakistan, had got involved in setting up a sugar mill in Hamira, a village near Jullundur (now Jalandhar), Punjab. Hence, we were saved from the horrible atrocities faced by millions fleeing across the newly declared international border at the time of the Partition, and we were there to provide shelter to several members of my father's family. Childhood was, therefore, spent in abnormal times when the nascent independent India was still struggling to redeem its 'tryst with destiny'. We, as children, never realised how difficult life must have been for our parents, as we were well insulated and protected. But, psychologically, we grew up to face adversity with confidence and realise the values of family.

English public schools were considered premier and were much sought-after educational institutions. My younger brothers, Rakesh and Rajive, and I started from Hampton Court, Mussoorie, which was adjoining an estate my grandfather had bought. Later, we went to Bishop Cotton School in Shimla, the oldest English public school established on the lines of Rugby and Marlboro. The school maintained its old traditions as an English public school and many of our senior teachers and housemasters were British. I belonged to the centenary batch which finished Senior Cambridge in the year 1959, when the school celebrated its centenary. The school's highest award was the President of India's Medal, given to the student who excelled in both academics as well as sports. I was awarded the President's Medal for the centenary year 1959, and it was the first and only time, the President personally gave the award.

After school, I went to St. Stephen's College, Delhi University—another minority institution run by a missionary and rated as the best college in India. The first Indian educational institution that I attended was the Faculty of Law, Delhi University; however, much of the law and codes we learnt were those we had inherited from the British. And when I joined the Indian Administrative Service, we still had at the helm the last vestiges of its predecessor, Imperial Civil Service.

My education and early stages of my career, therefore, spans over a period when Western influences were still rooted and India, as a nascent democracy, was administered by a civil service which was still transitioning from being primarily a revenue collection and maintaining law and order system to a development-oriented service in a democratic setup.

Although I was initially reluctant to join the Indian Administrative Service, it turned out to be a very diverse and rewarding experience. I underwent a metamorphosis early in my career and quite enjoyed the opportunities and challenges that I confronted during my tenure. The progression from the national to the international civil service, that is from state to central government in India and then transitioning to working with the United Nations, fulfilled my aspirations to deal with international relations and to carry the valuable experience I had gained at the national level to the international forum.

The anecdotal account of my career demonstrates that working in the national civil service can be a very challenging, but, nevertheless, a fulfilling life. It has also been my effort to remove any misconception that the life of a bureaucrat is straitlaced and devoid of any scope for taking initiative. While dealing with both development and law and order issues, it was possible to exercise discretion based on conviction and courage.

It is my hope that aspirants and new entrants into the civil service will find this book inspirational in building a successful and fulfilling career at both the national and international levels.

Ravi Sawhney

Acknowledgements

I acknowledge with gratitude the anonymous thousands in Punjab who kick-started my fulfilling life; the colleagues for their regard and support throughout my career; friends and family who have steadfastly stood by me and inspired me to write about living a meaningful life.

I also acknowledge with grateful thanks the very encouraging endorsements by Messrs Gopalakrishna Gandhi, N.N. Vohra, S.K. Misra and Nitin Desai as well as the initial guidance given by Ira Pande.

Acronyms

AC (UT)	Assistant Commissioners (Under Training)
AFTA	ASEAN Free Trade Area
APOs	Assistant Project Officers
APTA	Asia-Pacific Trade Agreement
ASEAN	Association of Southeast Asian Nations
BA (Hons)	Bachelor of Arts with Honours
BDOs	Block Development Officers
BIMSTEC	Bay of Bengal Initiative for Multi-Sectoral Technical and Economic Cooperation
BISTEC	Bangladesh, India, Sri Lanka and Thailand Economic Cooperation
BJP	Bharatiya Janata Party
BRI	Belt and Road Initiative
BRICS	Brazil-Russia-India-China-South Africa
CAREC	Central Asian Regional Economic Cooperation Programme
CCS	Cash Compensatory Support
DC	Deputy Commissioner
DFID	Department for International Development
ECO	Economic Cooperation Organization
ER	Economic Relations
ESCAP	Economic and Social Commission for Asia and the Pacific

GATT	General Agreement on Tariffs and Trade
GSP	Generalised System of Preferences
IAS	Indian Administrative Service
IFAD	International Fund for Agriculture Development
IFAS	International Fund for Saving the Aral Sea
IITF	India International Trade Fair
ISH	International Students House
JETRO	Japan External Trade Organization
LBSNAA	Lal Bahadur Shastri National Academy of Administration
MEA	Ministry of External Affairs
MFAL	Marginal Farmers and Agricultural Labourers Development Agency
MFN	Most Favoured Nation
MITI	Ministry of International Trade and Industry
NCDC	National Cooperative Development Corporation
PAU	Punjab Agriculture University
PSIDC	Punjab State Industrial Development Corporation
RCEP	Regional Comprehensive Economic Partnership
SAARC	South Asian Association for Regional Cooperation
SAFTA	South Asian Free Trade Area
SCO	Shanghai Cooperation Organisation
SFDA	Small Farmers Development Agency
SHGs	Self-Help Groups
SPECA	Special Programme for the Economies of Central Asia

SSP	Senior Superintendent of Police
UN	United Nations
UNECE	United Nations Economic Commission for Europe
UNOPS	United Nations Office for Project Services
WMPF	World Millennium Peace Foundation
WSSD	World Summit on Sustainable Development
WTO	World Trade Organization

1

A Reluctant Start

God gave us the gift of life;
it is up to us to give ourselves the gift of living well.
—Voltaire

I joined the Indian Administrative Service (IAS) in July 1968—that is more than half a century ago; in the last century; last millennium! It can, therefore, be expected that after such a long lapse of time, it will be difficult to precisely recall every detail or date of my career in the IAS and thereafter in the United Nations (UN). However, having spoken of some of the more significant events and incidents on several occasions, they remain fresh in my memory. Though suggestions were often made that I should document these interesting episodes in a book, I continued to procrastinate in spite of pressures from friends and family, particularly my wife Madhu and my children Ravina, Aushima and Raisa. As providence would have it, I fractured my ankle while playing golf and had to undergo surgery, as a result of which I am currently immobilized for the next few months. And so, out of this adversity came the opportunity to sit down to write my book on how I have lived my life.

Since a major part of my book will deal with experiences during my career in the IAS, it is only appropriate that I should first address the issue of my joining government service. Was my joining the IAS a fulfilment of my aspirations? The answer is 'No'. In fact, my joining the IAS was accidental. Unlike many others who had planned their careers in the IAS well in advance and accordingly planned their college education, I had no aspirations to join government service when I entered St. Stephen's College, Delhi. I applied for the BA (Hons) Economics course with no specific goal in mind. I recall Principal S.C. Sircar trying to persuade me during the interview to join one of the other honours courses since there were excessive applicants for the Economics course. I insisted, albeit without much conviction, that I wanted to do the Economics course. Eventually he agreed, probably because of my sports record. I found the course very dry and uninspiring, so I managed to graduate with a second division.

Sports, of course, was a different and more successful story. I did reasonably well in athletics representing the College, the University and at the Delhi State level as well as participating in some international competitions. My athletics career had started at Bishop Cotton School, Shimla, when in 1955 I broke seven school records in the Under 12 category. It was also the first time my name appeared in a newspaper. *The Tribune* reported on its sports page, 'Ravi Sawhney breaks seven school records in athletics'. The Victor Ladorum is an award given to the best athlete in each age category and I won it successively in the Under 12, Under 15 and the Open categories.

In college, I specialised in 400 metres, 400 metres hurdles and 4x400 metres relay. In view of my performance, when my younger brothers Rakesh and Rajive joined college, it was reported in the *Statesman* sports section, referring to my achievements in athletics. I recall being sent to Ceylon (now Sri Lanka) to participate in a dual athletic meet to run the 400 metres in place of the famous 'flying Sikh' Milkha Singh. There was a large crowd at the Colombo airport waiting with great excitement to receive Milkha Singh, especially after his historic performance at the Rome Olympics. When they were informed that I had come in place of Milkha, someone they had never heard of, there was understandable disappointment. I, therefore, felt a great sense of vindication when I beat their national champion in the 400 metres race in Kandy. For a while, Milkha and I had a common coach and it was he who arranged a spell of training for me along with Milkha at the National Stadium, Delhi, which was an unforgettable experience.

After graduation from St. Stephen's College, I had to start thinking of a career. In those days, the choice was quite limited. If one did not belong to a business family, the option was either to sit for the UPSC competitive examination for a government job, i.e., the IFS, IAS, IPS or one of the Central services, or join a firm which was then a very popular choice. If no other options were available, then try for a job in the tea estates. After a year's sabbatical spent planning on what I should do, I took my father's advice that a BA degree was not enough and I should study further, preferably law. He said even if I decided not to join the legal profession, knowledge of law would always be useful. This made eminent sense, so I joined the Faculty of Law, Delhi University. I stayed at the newly opened International Students House (ISH) which, as its name suggests, was meant to provide accommodation to foreign students. We were just two Indians there courtesy our warden Marr, who knew us when he was earlier at St. Stephen's College. The foreign students came from Thailand; South Africa, many of them were of Indian origin; Jordan; Egypt; one from the UAE with some links to the royal family; and from the Caribbean. Other than the Thais who tended to keep to themselves, probably because of language problem, we made friends with a cross-section of the students.

Life in the multicultural environment of ISH was an interesting exposure to the various foreign countries represented there. We had settled into a normal routine until one day in early 1965, Marr called me and said that he had invited Mrs Indira Gandhi, the then Minister of Information and Broadcasting, to meet the foreign students over dinner. He wanted me to sit next to her at dinner and try and persuade her to donate a television set to the hostel. In those days, television broadcasting was still in its primitive stage and owning a television set was rare. As planned, I sat next to Mrs Gandhi. She was in a very informal mood and regaled us with anecdotes of her travels with Pandit Nehru. In the course of conversation, she asked me how the foreign students had adjusted to living in India. I saw the opportunity and replied that generally they had settled down well but one thing they missed was the television. Then I suggested if she were to announce the donation of a television set to the hostel during her after-dinner speech, it would make them extremely happy. Mrs Gandhi smiled and told me to remind her.

During her speech, I tried to prompt Mrs Gandhi, whispering 'TV, TV,' but she seemed to pay no heed. I then tried by making an imprint of the word TV with a knife on the table cloth in front of her, as discreetly as I could, but then again, no response. When Mrs Gandhi finished her speech and sat down, I pointed out her omission to mention the television. She remarked that I should have reminded her and when I told her that I had, first by whispering and then pointing to the imprint of 'TV' which was still visible on the table cloth, Mrs Gandhi remarked, 'Oh, then you should have pinched me!' We had a great laugh but never got the television set.

In two years' time I had got an LLB degree, having topped the university in the final year. From there, it was a natural progression to the legal profession. After a brief internship, I joined one of the eminent corporate lawyers with international outreach, Kumar Shankardas. We had a very collegiate working relationship, based on good mutual understanding, especially with his very relaxed but efficient style of work. Having qualified for the LLB degree with merit and with an impressive record as an athlete, I was encouraged by some friends to apply for the Rhodes Scholarship in Oxford University. This scholarship is awarded to those who excel in both academics and sports. Unfortunately, I was not selected. I have often wondered what my life would have been had I gone to Oxford University – Would I have become an international athlete? Would I have joined the IAS? I do not think I will ever know.

While in the legal profession, I had started thinking of joining the Indian Foreign Service. My social circle included diplomats from several countries posted at their embassies in Delhi. Through my interaction with them, I got attracted to the diplomatic profession. I, therefore, simultaneously prepared for the competitive examinations. Unlike several of my contemporaries who had already chosen their career before joining college and accordingly selected the subjects to study, I faced the dilemma of having graduated in economics which, along with related subjects, was difficult to score in the competitive examinations. I, therefore, selected a combination of political science, constitutional history and law subjects. I got selected for the IAS instead of IFS which I had aimed for. It was one of those years when for some inexplicable reason, the intake into the Foreign Service was limited to just six vacancies, out of which, one was reserved for an ex-emergency commissioned army officer and a second for a Scheduled Caste candidate, leaving just four vacancies for the general category. I was high enough in the merit list to have qualified for the Foreign Service any other year when the intake was generally between 10 to 20 officers. The arbitrary nature of decision-making on annual quotas for the premier services became apparent when the intake in subsequent years was increased considerably to overcome the shortage of officers in the Foreign Service.

Not having seriously considered joining the IAS, I was not particularly enthused by the outcome and even contemplated not joining the service. Congratulatory messages and telegrams started pouring in and my father, quite understandably, was extremely happy that I had been selected for the IAS, then considered to be a highly prestigious service. When I indicated to my father that I was having second thoughts about joining the service, his advice was 'join the IAS and if you don't like it, you can always go back to the legal profession; but if you decide not to join, you might regret later and that option would no longer be there'. On the other hand, Kumar Shankardas tried his best to dissuade me from joining the service, as we were doing well together and he felt I had a great future in the legal profession. Once again, I thought my father's advice made eminent sense and so decided to join the IAS, and give it my best shot, not realising then that it is perhaps easier to join the service than to leave it. It is a profession, as I was to learn later, that affords immense opportunities to work in diverse areas, do the extraordinary and make a significant contribution to public service, as perhaps no other profession can.

2

Laying the Foundation

We know what we are, but know not what we may be.
—Shakespeare

The entire 1968 batch of all Central services entered Lal Bahadur Shastri National Academy of Administration (LBSNAA) that year and officially started their career as 'probationers', the term then used for trainees. While probationers from all the other services were there for just three months for the 'foundation course', before going to their respective training centres, the IAS probationers were there for almost a full year, before proceeding to their respective cadre states. The allocation of states was done on the basis of the listing of states in groups on a rotational basis. Vacancies in each state were filled on the basis of 50 per cent insiders, i.e., officers belonging to that state, and 50 per cent outsiders, i.e., officers from other states. If one was high enough on the merit list, the greater the chance of being allocated to one's home state. I was allocated to Punjab as per my choice even though it was not my home state. I was the senior most among the officers allocated to Punjab that year.

At the Academy, there were officers from every part of India, a few old friends and some familiar faces but a large majority were total strangers. And there was a huge diversity in backgrounds—engineers, teachers, lawyers, military, etc. and some straight from university. Soon, we all got to know each other and were on a first-name basis. The Academy, located in the premises of the erstwhile Charleville Hotel in Mussoorie, offers a salubrious setting, commanding breathtaking views of the Himalayas. The old colonial style complex had limited accommodation, thus requiring us to share rooms with vintage *hamams* for hot water and coal fireplaces. In its neighbourhood is the Happy Valley, inhabited largely by Tibetans. Their restaurants became popular for their *chang* (rice wine) and *momos* (dumplings).

Mussoorie for me was the place where I spent my early childhood. My grandfather had a large estate, the Grange, which was the summer holiday home for the entire family. My schooling started in Hampton Court School which was above the Grange, separated by just a road. In 1953, my parents decided to send me and my younger brother Rakesh to Bishop Cotton School, Shimla where we completed our school education. The summer vacations in Mussoorie resumed only after finishing school and joining college in Delhi.

In 2018, the 1968 batch was invited by the Academy to celebrate our 'Golden Jubilee', marking 50 years of our joining the service. For those like me who had not visited the Academy for years, the Academy complex had undergone an unbelievable change. After a fire destroyed the main building, the entire complex was rebuilt and transformed from the old vintage colonial complex to a modern luxurious complex. Residential buildings with five-star facilities and meeting rooms with full conference facilities were indeed most impressive. The only old building remaining was the Director's office. I had mixed feelings—though the nostalgia was lost, the change with added facilities was remarkable. The change was not just in the Academy complex but also in the appearance of batchmates. We had all aged and quite understandably so, after more than 50 years! But some were quite unrecognizable, having perhaps allowed themselves to age uncontrollably. Fortunately, name tags saved many from the embarrassment of not recognizing and asking, 'Who are you?' Nevertheless, it was a most memorable get-together that had us reminiscing about our days as probationers.

While we were all filled with nostalgia, the irony was not lost that several of us had first met as aspiring probationers and now were meeting again as retirees! Many had distinguished themselves and could look back on a career with legitimate pride and satisfaction. To mention a few are Vineeta Rai, who had many firsts to her credit as Secretary in the Central government, Mohan Kanda, who from a child star became the Chief Secretary of Andhra Pradesh, Vivek Agnihotri as Secretary General of the Rajya Sabha and Wajahat Habibullah as the first Chief Information Commissioner under the RTI Act. Some from other services are Ambassador Aftab Seth (IFS) as Ambassador to Japan and Ajit Doval (IPS), currently serving as National Security Advisor. Perhaps the most prominent is Gopalkrishna Gandhi who distinguished himself as High Commissioner to South Africa and Sri Lanka, Secretary to President of India and Governor of West Bengal.

Incidentally, the term 'probationer' is no longer used because of the realisation that it had a negative connotation. The new recruits are now referred to as 'officers under training'.

As probationers, life in the Academy was quite busy, with an early morning start doing the Canadian Air Force exercises (5BX). I was one of the PT leaders, selected on the basis of perceived physical fitness. Horse riding was compulsory, though a traumatic experience for many. 'If you can't sit on a horse, how will you administer a district,' shouted Nawal Singh with his handlebar moustache to anyone found wobbling on the saddle. Of course, riding is no longer prevalent in the districts but it became a test of overcoming fear and so was an essential part of the training programme for IAS trainees. At the end of the year, there was competition for the best rider and the most physically fit probationer. I was awarded the Director's medal for physical fitness. Deputy Prime Minister Morarji Desai visited the Academy and awarded the medals.

The faculty in the Academy was a mix of professional teachers and government officers of varying seniorities, so we could get the benefit of both the theoretical and practical aspects of public administration. There were some probationers who very assiduously attended the lectures, aiming to score well in the final examination and thereby improve their rank in the merit list. They came to be known as 'KTPs' … keen type probationers!

Recreation on the premises included billiards and bridge. I favoured the former. A popular pastime in the evenings was a walk to the mall, sitting at 'Whispering Windows' and sipping an aperitif, watching the world go by. The Tibetan cafes were also popular for those who relished *momos* washed down by jugs full of *chang*. Thanks to our ex-army colleagues, we could get rum at affordable prices from the military canteen in Dehradun. It was a popular drink as one could still be ready for PT next morning without a hangover. There were also the occasional formal dinners when we had to wear our black *bandgallas* and behave suitably. The exception, I recall, was during Christmas when the festivities and fun were not hampered by our formal attire. I remember Mussoorie had once the heaviest snowfall over the Christmas week. I had hosted a party at my grandfather's house and the snowfall was so heavy that we could not return to the Academy till early next morning, wading through knee-deep snow. Fortunately, there was no PT that morning.

I had a car while at the Academy. Invariably over the long weekend, normally the second Saturday, I would drive down to Delhi on Friday evening, party with my friends over the weekend and then leave Delhi just after midnight on Sunday to be back at the Academy in time for PT on Monday morning. Thinking back, it was a crazy thing to do but can best be explained away as youthful exuberance.

Military attachment was an integral part of our training programme, the rationale being that such exposure to military life would be useful for public administration, especially in times of extreme law and order situations when the military might need to be called to assist the civil administration. We were sent in small groups to different military units across the country. My group was attached to the 3rd Dogra Battalion, stationed in Daranga on the India-Bhutan border. During the three weeks we were there, we followed the Battalion's regular routine, starting with an early morning road run followed by breakfast, lectures and then a visit to the Officers' Mess for gimlet before lunch. I do not recall enjoying gimlet as much as I did then.

Our training also included the use of firearms, especially the sophisticated automatic weapons, which was something exciting to look forward to. The 8th Armoured Division commanded by Brig. Rodney Hira was stationed nearby in Rangia (Assam) and we were taken there to witness a demonstration of the full firepower of the Division. Little did I know then that years later I would be meeting Brig. Hira again as a Lieutenant General when the issue of military assistance to civil administration would actually arise in Punjab.

Historically, Daranga was part of a major trade route to Bhutan and the venue of an annual festival when traders would converge from all over to indulge in festivities. Unfortunately, this also attracted people in the flesh trade and soon this place became notorious for it. Gradually, settlements came up on the no-man's land, a 400-metre strip of land with a rivulet flowing through it. They were, therefore, outside the control of both countries but also with no access to healthcare. Keeping the army jawans away was a difficult problem that posed a serious threat to their health and hygiene. 'When crossing the no-man's land into Bhutan, don't even look at them,' warned Col Tiwari on the very first day. We could walk into Bhutan freely and visit a nearby post office. I was amazed to see how attractive Bhutanese postage stamps were. A delight for anyone interested in philately.

Our training culminated in a Bharat Darshan. We were sent in groups to different parts of the country, ostensibly to understand and appreciate the rich and diverse cultural heritage of our country. My group started with Maharashtra where we visited the ancient Ajanta and Ellora caves; a visit, as I recall, to Jalgaon district to witness the 'Levy Day' function; and the state secretariat. This was followed by visits to Goa and the southern states, Andhra Pradesh, Mysore (Karnataka) and Madras (Tamil Nadu). Visits to see the holy relics of the 16th century Spanish missionary St Francis Xavier, the beautiful carvings in temples in Halebidu and Belur, the Salar Jung Museum in Hyderabad and the Vivekananda Rock in Kanyakumari will remain etched in my memory forever.

3

Getting into the Groove

Take up one idea. Make that one idea your life — think of it, dream of it, live on that idea. Let the brain, muscles, nerves, every part of your body, be full of that idea, and just leave every other idea alone. This is the way to success.

—Swami Vivekananda

PUNJAB

Five of us, including an ex-army officer and one belonging to the reserved category (SC), were allocated to the Punjab cadre. Two were insiders and three including me were from outside the state. We were designated as Assistant Commissioners (Under Training) or ACs (UT). Our first assignment was to attend the Punjab Revenue Training School in Chandigarh for training in land revenue law and administration. The school was in a modest house including training and residential facilities. The trainer was an expert whose voice at most times was inaudible. It was also a great opportunity for the cadre mates to bond. After the initial training covering land revenue documents maintained at the village, kanungo circle, tehsil and district levels, we were sent for practical training in deciding land mutation cases, albeit limited to uncontested cases. We had to be watchful that a wily patwari did not get the disputed cases decided in this process. I did my practical tehsil level training in Patiala. With a number of old friends in and around Patiala, Chandigarh, Mandi Ahmedgarh and Ambala, it was a wonderful time to catch up with them.

AMRITSAR

I was sent to Amritsar for the next phase of our training at the district level. I arrived in Amritsar and went directly to report to K.S. Bains, Deputy Commissioner (DC), belonging to the 1962 batch. With Akali government in power and his father-in-law being an active member, Bains carried some political clout to reinforce his reputation as an effective administrator. I was surprised when he told me that two ACs (UT), belonging to the 1967 batch, were still undergoing district training. This was unusual as the rest of their batch was already posted in sub-divisions as Sub Divisional Officer (Civil), normally the first substantive posting for IAS officers. I could detect there was a hiatus in the relationship between Bains and the two trainees. This was later confirmed when I met them. It was also the reason why Bains regarded me with a certain amount of scepticism. He told me to report to his office the next day where a training programme would be provided to me.

With regard to my stay, Bains informed me that Karl Reddy, one of the two trainees, had offered to share his accommodation with me. The traditional practice of DCs providing boarding to trainees in their own residence had been discarded long before, ostensibly for economic reasons but more so to maintain their privacy. I accompanied Karl to his residence, which he said was inaccessible by car and so I had to park my car at a nearby road. I soon understood, to my utter shock, why his home had no vehicular access. Karl had rented a room in the subzi mandi (vegetable market) with access to the public toilet! I spent the night there feeling totally disillusioned. The next morning when I reported to Bains, I explained my plight to him. He was kind enough to allot me a room in the Circuit House, albeit not in the main building but in a run-down annexe. Anyway, this was far better than being in the subzi mandi, so I settled in with a sigh of relief and gratitude.

The customary training during district attachment is to spend time in every branch in the Deputy Commissioner's office and observe its functioning. One also sat in as an observer in the district level meetings. Some work might be gradually allotted, depending upon the impression one made on the DC. In those days, one of the more important government programmes was to encourage farmers to use chemical fertilizers. District level targets were fixed which were further disaggregated to the development block level. Periodic meetings were held to review the progress in achieving the targets and even to exceed them. Given the priority, this programme was an important barometer of effective district administration. In one of my periodic training review sessions with Bains, we discussed this programme. By now, I had made some impression on the DC about my earnestness and so he was ready to give some special attention to my training. I evinced interest in undergoing field training as I felt just sitting in the office as an observer was getting quite boring. Bains suggested that I spend some time visiting villages and interacting with farmers to understand how they viewed such programmes in particular and the work of the district administration in general.

An Agriculture Inspector was deputed to accompany me, and I spent about two weeks touring villages in Amritsar district and interacting with the rural community, including farmers, rural school teachers, sarpanches, panches, etc. It was an invaluable experience at the grassroots level to understand how the targeted beneficiaries viewed government's rural development schemes at the district level and the work of government functionaries at different levels. The main focus of the Green Revolution was to encourage farmers to use phosphatic fertilizers and urea for which monthly targets were set for each development block. It appeared that while the extension staff concentrated more on the larger and more influential farmers, the smaller farmers had been marginalised. Hence, even though targets were being met, equitable distribution of fertilizer was neglected. Consequently, a more disaggregated system of reporting was introduced with separate focus on small/marginal farmers.

The hospitality meted out was simple but genuine. Nights would be spent in whichever village I happened to be, hosted by either a sarpanch or a school teacher or just a generous farmer. The weather was conducive to sleeping out in the open under the starlit sky. At times, the choicest local brew, rich in dry fruits, would be brought out with hard-boiled eggs, and sitting around a fire, we would have an open and frank discussion. Bains was very appreciative of my insightful report as the traditional system in district administration, being more a top-down approach and essentially target-oriented, had failed to assess the actual benefit to the target groups, especially the more vulnerable sections of the rural population. I believe this kind of exposure and experience should become an integral part of training at the district level to bring about qualitative improvement in district administration. By now, I had developed a good rapport with the DC, so he readily agreed to my request to earmark a house in a new government housing colony for ACs (UT). Some basic furniture was also provided. I became the first occupant of this house.

Another memorable episode, again, off the beaten track, during this period in Amritsar was my appointment as an Administrator of a college. The management committee of Guru Teg Bahadur College, located in village Sathiala, had members owing allegiance to both the Akali and Jan Sangh parties. The committee had become non-functional due to irreconcilable dispute between the two groups. On the recommendation of the DC, the Akali government decided to take over the management of the college, much to the chagrin of the Jan Sangh group. A majority of the faculty was supportive of the Jan Sangh group and so was opposed to the takeover by the government. I was appointed Administrator with the responsibility to ensure that the examinations, which were due in about two months, were held on time. I camped in the PWD Rest House, Rayya, which is a mandi town about 10 km from Sathiala. As I did not have a government vehicle, I used my own car to commute to Sathiala.

I arrived at the college to a very hostile environment. The staff committee representing the opposing group had decided to boycott me and passed a resolution to fine any staff member who greeted me, leave alone meeting me. A few days later, I was informed that some staff members were provoking students to stone my car in protest against the takeover. There were also reports of alcohol being distributed to student leaders to win their support in opposing the takeover. My primary responsibility was to ensure law and order be maintained for the normal functioning of the college so that examinations could be held as scheduled. After a week or so, the atmosphere continued to be tense with no solution in sight.

One afternoon, I stood in my office looking out of the window watching students playing sports. Some were playing football, some volleyball and some athletes running around the track. Then I noticed a few students practicing hurdles and having been a 400-metres hurdler myself, I noticed that they lacked the basic technique to cross hurdles. So, I strolled down to the field, went across to them and offered to coach them. Fortunately, they were very receptive and this became a daily routine. Within a few days, a rapport had been established not only with the budding hurdlers but also with other sportsmen who had observed with keen interest my efforts to coach. The ice had been broken and I could sense the growing respect for me, even though initially as a fellow sportsman. As sportsmen command considerable respect and invariably become natural leaders in educational institutions, the salutary effect of this bonding with them was the creation of a support base in my favour among the student community. Now the recalcitrant staff members found themselves marginalised. The message from the student community to them was very clear that their opposition and provocations would no longer be tolerated. It was smooth going thereafter and examinations were held as scheduled.

During this assignment, I went through another very unique and totally unrelated experience. I had been camping in Rayya when an emissary from the head of the Radha Soami Dera in Beas came to meet me. Maharaj Charan Singh ji had got to know that I was appointed Administrator and was camping in Rayya. I had met him some years ago when one of my old school friends Karanbir Singh Sandhu (Guddu) got married to Maharaj ji's niece, Laddi. The wedding took place in Beas and I was part of a small *baraat* (the groom's wedding procession). The message from Maharaj ji was simple, 'Why are you staying in a rest house when you can stay in the Dera? You are family.' I was so pleasantly surprised by Maharaj ji's invitation and recalling the amazing hospitality that had been extended to us earlier, I readily accepted. I was given accommodation in the international hostel where Maharaj ji's followers from all over the world were staying. Among them were many celebrities including, as I learnt over breakfast one morning sitting next to me, was a Hollywood actress who had acted in one of Elvis Presley's movies. There were also some familiar faces who were understandably surprised to see me. 'We didn't know you were a follower of Radha Soami!' would be the usual remark.

Maharaj ji would come to the international hostel every evening and give a discourse, which was listened to with rapt attention. I noted that the expressions of many of his followers were like that of one who had just seen God. Some would even be moved to tears. Breakfast would be served early morning and talk at the table of four/five persons would revolve around *simran* (meditation) and *sewa* (selfless service). As I had no contribution to make to the conversation, it became embarrassing to confess that I was not a follower. One day, I asked to meet Maharaj ji to explain my predicament. I said that I felt guilty misusing his Dera, also confessing that my lunch at the college was usually non-vegetarian. Maharaj ji looked at me and said smilingly, 'I have not asked you to be a Radha Soami. You are here because you are family.'

To ease my own mind and out of curiosity, I decided to know more about the Radha Soami philosophy. I read Julian Johnson's book *Path of the Masters* which was very illuminating. He explains that it is not a different religion but a method of realisation of God through the medium of a living Guru. *Simran* based on a *jaap* (chanting) given by Maharaj ji and *sewa* were essential practices. I had myself witnessed scores of followers carrying heavy loads on their heads, some so old that you would think they needed support to walk, doing *sewa*, and that too, without the slightest sign of strain. Maybe the *darshan* of

Maharaj ji, who would be sitting there, gave them this unimaginable strength. It is an amazing feat that the Dera has been built largely through *sewa*. Having completed my assignment as Administrator, I left the Dera, feeling a sense of satisfaction over the experience but not to the extent to consider becoming a Radha Soami.

I had heard of Pingalwara in Amritsar, an institution devoted to the care of the homeless and destitute, which was started by Bhagat Puran Singh, who had migrated to Amritsar during the Partition. A visit to the shelter revealed not only the extreme physical suffering of humanity but also the shocking callousness meted to such suffering. The Pingalwara movement was an ode to the man who undertook to look after those who had been abandoned by their families or had no one to look after them due to their physical infirmities. I felt his mission was as noble and charitable as that of Mother Teresa, but unfortunately, with far less recognition and support.

At the time of the Partition, Bhagat Puran Singh discarded all his material belongings and instead carried a lame man, a stranger, on his shoulders across the border to Amritsar. He looked after him and gradually the number of physically challenged, who came into his fold, increased. To collect donations, boxes were kept in public places like bus stands in the city. Donations also came in kind like baskets of food being left in the Pingalwara, some by families of inmates, perhaps to ease their conscience for abandoning them. I was so moved by what I saw that I discussed with the DC on how to get Bhagat Puran Singh greater recognition. We decided to recommend his name for a national award. I wrote out a citation recommending him for a Padma Shri award, describing him as the modern-day 'Good Samaritan' but unfortunately, it was in vain.

Social life in Amritsar was very hectic. I already knew some families and through them, I became part of a very active social circle within a very short time. 'Amritsaris' are known for their hospitality and their fondness for good food and 'drinks'! Lavish parties were frequent. Toshi and Brij Monga opened their home to me and virtually became my family in Amritsar. Among my friends with whom I spent many an enjoyable evening, were Miki and Puni, posted in the Grindlays Bank branch at Amritsar. It was such a pleasure to spend time in their tastefully furnished home and enjoy their warm hospitality. Another couple, SC and Sushma, epitomized the best kind of hospitality that Amritsar is famous for and I spent many an evening with them.

There was a group of young golfers who played at the army course, which had 'browns' not 'greens'. I got initiated into golf but played very infrequently due to my work commitments outside Amritsar. The same group was also into playing bridge. I had played bridge earlier but my knowledge of conventions was very rudimentary. It became a great pastime and we had bridge sessions that extended through a whole weekend. I recall with some amusement, one day I got a telephone call in the office. The caller was Uma Binode Singh, the sister of my very close school friends, Mukhi and Sukhi, and married into one of the most reputed and aristocratic families in Amritsar. She had planned bridge that morning at her home but one of her friends could not come, reducing them to just three. Hence, the frantic call to me to come help out the three 'ladies in distress'. I was obviously disinclined initially, but eventually succumbed and joined them. After that the story went around the city that if anyone is ever caught in such a situation and needs a fourth hand for bridge, I was available to bail them out! Another memorable episode was my accepting an invitation from Government College for Women to attend a function as chief guest. I lost my anonymity and after that wherever I went I could see fingers pointing towards me. It was flattering but also at times embarrassing.

My stint in Amritsar was both enriching in experience and enjoyable, cementing old friendships and making some new ones that have lasted till today. The 1970 New Year eve bash was memorable for not just the fantastic food, dancing to rocking music but also as my last night in Amritsar. Early on New Year's Day, 1971, I loaded my car and drove to Hoshiarpur where I had been posted as SDM.

4

The Metamorphosis

Life's most persistent and urgent question is,
'What are you doing for others?'
—Martin Luther King Jr.

As I drove down to Hoshiarpur, I wondered what it would be like as I had never visited it before. Amritsar had been a good experience as I had friends there and it was easy to settle in. I knew no one in Hoshiarpur. But then there was the excitement of going to my first substantive posting. As I drove into town, it appeared less developed than Amritsar and there was far less hustle-bustle. I found my way to the Circuit House, as this was where I would be staying till my predecessor vacated the SDM's house.

Hoshiarpur district is part of the Doaba region of Punjab and its ancient history indicates it was part of the Indus Valley Civilisation. Before the Partition, it was an important centre for education as well as the trade route from Punjab to Kangra and Una in the Shiwalik Hills, now in Himachal Pradesh. While Amritsar, Jullundur and Ludhiana were industrially developed, Hoshiarpur remained in a time-warp. To encourage industry, the Punjab government had declared it industrially backward and offered special incentives for development in the district. This, however, had no positive impact as the lack of infrastructure and problems relating to its topography far outweighed the incentives offered.

Hoshiarpur was notorious for its *choes* and *chowdaries* and its 'cooks and crooks'! Most of the *choes* (seasonal rivulets), coming down from the *kandi* (sub-mountainous) belt, had no fixed course. However, the bigger ones could be canalised with bridges over them to facilitate movement of traffic. A large number of small rivulets crisscrossing the roads posed a challenge every monsoon, especially as their course and duration were unpredictable. When they were in spate, one had to wait, sometimes for hours, to let the water abate. There was an engineer who had drawn up a grandiose plan to canalise all the major *choes* and conserve the water for irrigation, but it never got implemented. Chowdary Balbir Singh, the local Jan Sangh MLA, epitomised the infamous *chowdaries* of Hoshiarpur. He was notorious for his maverick behaviour and theatrics in meetings. I recall in one district meeting he was complaining about the quality of water and took off his saffron turban to show there was sand on his bald head. As for 'cooks and crooks', I had a very good cook but did not really come across anyone beyond the usual kind of crooks one would find in any place.

Hoshiarpur is also a very famous centre of astrology since the *Bhrigu Samhita*, a treatise dictated by sage Bhrigu over 5,000 years ago and believed to be the final word in astrology, is located there. The Bhrigu Samhita complex here has attracted people in droves from all parts of the country and even from abroad.

T.K.A. Nair, better known as Kutty Nair, from Kerala and of the 1963 IAS batch, was the Deputy Commissioner of Hoshiarpur. His boyish looks and unassuming demeanour led many to mistakenly think he was the son of the DC. But Kutty Nair had gained respect and reputation for his integrity and clarity of mind which more than compensated for his 'non-Punjabiness'. His informal demeanour in our very first meeting was very comforting and we maintained a very cordial relationship throughout. About a year later, Kutty Nair was succeeded by V.K. Khanna of the same batch. He came from a business family in Amritsar. His easy-going ways could at times be misconstrued for complacency or even disinterest.

I settled in my work as an SDM, including dealing with land revenue, administration of court work, matters relating to law and order and rural development. Weekly overnight tours were an essential, but interesting part of my work. These tours were necessary to review the rural development work on the ground as well as to undertake work related to land revenue administration. Although land revenue was no longer a significant source of income for the government, the maintenance of accurate land revenue records right down to the village level was, and remained, a very important responsibility. These tours also broke the monotony of office work, especially as some of the rest houses in the subdivision were located in remote, deeply forested sub-mountainous areas. My favourite rest houses were at Bunga and Dholbaha, especially after I had started to combine some of my tours with *shikar* (hunting), as game like partridge and wild boar was abundant in the adjoining areas. Dholbaha had traces of several ancient historical and architectural sites, including remains of temples scattered across the area.

One Shivratri, which was a holiday, I was lazing at home with nothing in particular to do when a message came that there was a dispute in a village which could turn ugly and even violent. When I arrived at the village, there was considerable tension and threat of violence breaking out. The ostensible reason was very disturbing. Drain water from some houses inhabited by scheduled caste villagers was overflowing into areas and drains in front of the neighbouring, higher caste *Jat* houses. The matter was more complex as from the ensuing discussion it was apparent that tension had been building up between a few people from the two groups because of other reasons and the drainage issue was just the breaking point. After considerable effort and persuasion and veiled threat of punitive action, we were able to resolve the matter amicably. The village *sarpanch* had undertaken to ensure that the drains were kept clean and not clogged with waste which had caused the drains to overflow.

On the return journey, we passed the Bhrigu Samhita complex and my security guard suggested that we drop in as the priests there had been repeatedly requesting me to visit them. As it was a holiday and I had no other plans, I agreed and we arrived there unannounced. Pandit Janardhan came out to welcome me. As I had not given any thought to his earlier requests to visit, I said I had dropped in out of sheer curiosity. In the process of explaining to me and amplifying by using my birth details, Pandit Janardhan revealed to me that they had found my *janam kundli* (horoscope). He showed me some small sheets of parchment paper with text written in Sanskrit, wrapped in cellophane. He pulled out the top sheet and started reading it to me. It was a dialogue between Sage Bhrigu and his disciple Shukra starting with the question that if someone is born on my specific date and time of birth, what his life would be like. The answer was that this *balak* (child) would be named Ravi and he would come to the

Bhrigu Samhita complex on Shivratri. I could decipher this bit and in a state of startled disbelief, I excused myself saying I would come back again to have the *kundli* read in full. Not being a strong believer in astrological matters, a year or so passed and I had not returned to Bhrigu Samhita complex. But a number of people I knew, including some friends, came to Hoshiarpur just to have their fortunes told. The *kundli* could be either a *janam kundli* based on a person's date and time of birth or *prashan kundli*, which was based on a specific question for which a person comes for a consultation. Several people would come during the same two-hour span when the *prashan kundli* would be taken up and only one would be lucky enough to get an answer.

There was considerable folklore about the *Bhrigu Samhita*. One heard of a case where a person driving into Hoshiarpur had asked someone the way to the Bhrigu Samhita complex. The local person offered to accompany him in the car as he lived near the complex. This visitor found his *kundli* and it mentioned the name of the person who had accompanied him! However, not everyone would find his *kundli*. Apparently, a large number pages of the collection were destroyed by a tea shop owner, who, not knowing what the parchment papers were, was using them to wrap sweets till one day Pandit Des Raj happened to visit the tea shop and discovered their authenticity and value. He retrieved whatever he could and brought the lot to Hoshiarpur, where he, along with his sons, set up the Bhrigu Samhita complex.

I had been in Hoshiarpur for a year or so when my parents came to visit me. My mother, of course, had heard about the Bhrigu Samhita complex and was impatient to visit the place. Her main concern was when I was going to get married. My youngest brother, Rajive, had already got married and I was not showing any great inclination to settle down. Hence, her anxiety, especially as my maternal uncle who was also in the IAS and very close to me, remained a confirmed bachelor. When I told her that I had already visited the place, found my *kundli* but had not had the full *kundli* read, it heightened her impatience to visit there as early as possible.

So, on the next holiday, we went to the Bhrigu Samhita complex. Pandit Janardhan received us and he read out the entire *kundli.* There was the obvious reference to my being involved in administration and dispensing justice and generalities about my life in future. That did not impress me as these were matters that were public knowledge or could be easily deduced therefrom. But what was completely startling and left me in stunned disbelief was the disclosure that my father had been born in the family of Bishen Dass Kohli but would carry forward the name of Pratap Singh Sawhney's family. My father had been adopted as a child by his uncle who had no children. It was not something I had discussed with anyone nor was it a matter that could have been found out during a background check. Thus, the veracity of the *kundli* had been clearly established. As for my getting married, it did confirm that I would get married and to someone whose name started with 'M'. I married Madhu a few years later. It was also indicated that I would change my profession later in life. This, too, happened when I took premature voluntary retirement from the IAS to work with the UN.

In December 1971, the War of Liberation started in East Pakistan and soon India was involved in a war with Pakistan on the western front. Although Hoshiarpur is not a border district, it was close to the action, especially as the Adampur Air Force station was nearby. We had to enforce blackouts and remain on constant alert as the noise of sirens and bomb explosions was a frequent occurrence, particularly during the night. On a moonlit night, the enemy planes were reportedly guided to their target, the Adampur air base, by following the glistening train tracks and would circle over Hoshiarpur. After a few days, we received a report of a Pakistani plane having been shot down near Hoshiarpur. On reaching the site, we saw a two-seater plane that had virtually crash-landed on its nose. It was an executive plane used for transporting senior-most military officers. There was one survivor and the body of the pilot was lying nearby. The survivor was a Bengali officer who had hitched a ride in the absence of any senior army officer, and had hijacked the plane forcing the pilot to turn towards India. As per his statement, there was resistance from the pilot leading to a mid-air scuffle during which he shot the pilot, forcing the crash-landing. We took the officer into custody and immediately informed appropriate authorities in the state government. News of this incident spread across the town and immediately there was a strong public demand to honour the survivor and to take him out in a public procession for his bravery in hijacking a Pakistani plane. This was understandably disallowed and the officer was kept in custody till the authorities concerned took charge of him. After this incident, reportedly all Bengali officers who remained in West Pakistan became suspect and were kept under close surveillance and many in custody.

The war was soon over with the surrender of the Pakistan Army and the liberation of Bangladesh. Life in Hoshiarpur became normal again. Unlike in Amritsar, there was virtually no socially like-minded company in Hoshiarpur. Fortunately, the Civil Services Club, very close to my residence, had tennis courts and I became part of a regular foursome. Kapila *sahib*, a retired civil servant, who must have then been in his late seventies, still played tennis very energetically. His son Ramesh Kapila was much senior to me in the Punjab government and it was an amusing sight to see him being treated like an adolescent by his father whenever he visited the club. Ramesh Kapila would just smile it away with a hint of embarrassment. Then there were a couple of professors from Government College, Bawa Sahib and Virender Kumar (VK). They were also regular rummy players, so playing rummy with them along with Dr Goel, with his double MD degrees, became our regular pastime in the evenings. The stakes were nominal and the maximum one could lose in an evening was Rs 5. As I was not particularly good at it nor serious about playing cards, I was the most frequent loser, inviting the quip, 'Why do you bother to come to the club, just send Rs 5 every evening'!

Kutty Nair was not the club going kind, so was never seen there except when there was some function. During my time there, I was able to procure a billiard table for the club. Satbir Singh (Sunny Jind), the former Maharaja of Jind and a very close friend, was selling some household goods of his former palace in Sangrur. He informed me about the billiard table on which we had previously played a few times was up for sale. I visited Sangrur and bought the billiard table along with brass chandeliers, benches, cues, some of which had ivory handles and were autographed by famous players, and two boxes of billiard balls for the club. For most club members, this was the first time they played billiards. It soon became popular. However, I believe that after I left Hoshiarpur, the table was more frequently used for laying out eats for tea parties!

While there were not many like-minded people in Hoshiarpur, I did make some wonderful friends. Apart from my tennis and rummy groups, there were two families in particular with whom I spent memorable times. One was that of Sardar Harbans Singh, Chaunniwala, a highly respected and well-known personality. Though much older to me, we drew very close and he became my well-wisher. His farmlands were very close to the town and he had gained fame for horticulture development, particularly kinnow oranges and juicy mangoes. His hospitality was renowned and one could enjoy it fully in an uninhibited manner knowing he had no ulterior motive. Many an evening was spent in his farm, enjoying kinnow orange juice in winter and buckets-full of mangoes in summer. Hoshiarpur was famous for these fruits. The other family was the amiable Dr Chowdhary and his family, who were always pleasant company. I also had some very good school friends living close to Hoshiarpur. Among them were Bali and his wife Vijaya, who lived in Mandi Ahmedgarh, less than a two-hour drive from Hoshiarpur. We spent some memorable evenings together at his farm. One that stands out most was when we celebrated his son Amarinder's first birthday soon after I arrived in Hoshiarpur. It was a party that actually extended from the birthday evening to the next day and when I eventually returned to the Circuit House there was a group of office staff, anxiously waiting for me to conduct court work.

Sardar Harbans Singh's elder son Buggal was a very keen *shikari* and so we frequently went shooting, either for partridges and pheasants or for bigger game like deer and wild boar. There was a tribal village inhabited by *shikligars* whose traditional metalcraft was to make knives, spearheads, etc. They were also traditionally into hunting especially wild boar, using well-trained dogs and nets. They were quite fearless. If a boar escaped the shooters and got entangled in a net, they would wrestle with it and bring it under their control. We used their expertise in tracking wild boar. Just after a rainfall when hoof-marks would be fresh, they could track the herd with almost pinpoint accuracy even in the difficult hilly terrain. The hunt would be conducted with dogs whose keen noses will detect the presence of boars and track the scent. Their loud barking would alert us that a boar would be exiting out into the open any moment. It was always a successful hunt and wild boar pickle was a regular on the menu.

There was, however, a brief interlude in the rather sedate social group one had reconciled to. A newly recruited IAS officer arrived for his district training with his wife—Amitabh and Ira Pande. They were cherubic and chubby, and very cheerful in both appearance and demeanour. From our very first meeting, we bonded instantly, a bond which lasts even today, even after more than 50 years! As related by them, when they alighted at the bus stand wearing traditional colourful attire, they heard murmurs out of curiosity whether a circus was coming to town! During their brief stay in Hoshiarpur, my parents happened to be visiting me and they developed an instant attachment to both Amitabh and Ira, and they soon became part of our family. Ira was a wonderful company for my mother and together they went on interesting trips to places of religious significance, such as the holy shrine in Chintpurni.

The antiquity of Hoshiarpur is known to be identified with the Harrapan period. During one of these *shikar* outings in the remote areas of the Shiwalik Hills near Dholbaha, we came across scattered ruins of an ancient temple, hitherto undiscovered and, therefore, unprotected by the government archaeology agencies. Beautifully carved stone statues and sculptures, probably of the medieval period, were scattered all over, fortunately still undiscovered by indiscriminate dealers. These valuable relics were retrieved and displayed as museum pieces in the Sadhu Ashram in Hoshiarpur, which houses the renowned Vishveshvaranand Vishwa Bandhu Institute of Sanskrit and Indological Studies.

My tenure as SDM was less than a year. I was reposted at Hoshiarpur on a different assignment. The Government of India had launched a new rural development programme under which agencies to implement the programme were set up in selected districts in every state. The programme was designed to assist marginal farmers (holding less than one hectare of land) and landless agricultural labourers through the creation of supplementary occupation, and similarly in some districts for small farmers. The former was called the Marginal Farmers and Agricultural Labourers Development Agency (MFAL) and the other, Small Farmers Development Agency (SFDA). Punjab was allocated two SFDA and two MFAL projects covering four districts. Hoshiarpur district was selected for MFAL and I was appointed the Project Director.

The main objective of this programme was to provide supplementary sources of income to the economically vulnerable sections of the rural population through schemes such as dairy, poultry and pig farming. Other schemes included assistance in providing pumps for irrigation and creation of supplementary employment for landless agricultural labourers, especially during the lean season. The assistance was in the form of bank loans at differential rates of interest together with a subsidy of 33 per cent. For the small farmers, owning more than one hectare, but less than two hectares, the subsidy component was 25 per cent. In the initial phase, the target beneficiaries were to be identified and a database of potential beneficiaries was to be created. This was by its very nature a time-consuming process, and reportedly took agencies across the country almost a year to complete.

In Hoshiarpur, I had followed a slightly different implementation process. We adopted a more innovative approach. Instead of focusing on only identifying the target beneficiaries in the entire district, we identified the target group in every village and immediately formed them into a cooperative society for dairy, poultry or pig farming, depending upon their interest. I had two former Block Development Officers (BDOs) as Assistant Project Officers (APOs). I instructed them to remain in the field and achieve the targets given to them within the specified time. I was not going to monitor their whereabouts or working hours but expected them to report to me once every week with details of the work done.

Hence, while other districts were still in the process of completing the identification of potential beneficiaries, we had simultaneously started implementation of schemes. Dairy farming was the more popular scheme. The target beneficiaries were taken to popular cattle fairs called *mandis* in Punjab to purchase buffaloes of good pedigree, accompanied by a team comprising a loan officer from the bank, a veterinary doctor and an APO under my direct supervision. The entire process of procurement would be completed at the fair itself—the selection of the buffalo by the farmer, its check-up by the veterinary doctor and the processing of the loan for direct payment to the seller as well as simultaneously crediting the 33 per cent subsidy to the buyer's account. All buffaloes purchased were stamped to obviate any chance of the same buffalo being resold at another fair. It was a fascinating experience notwithstanding all the dirt, especially during the monsoon season, that one can expect in a cattle fair. One could actually discern tangible benefit being passed on, something not common in most government schemes. In a few months, we had set up a number of dairy cooperative societies and village link roads from major roads in the district were dotted with signboards, 'MFAL DAIRY COOPERATIVE SOCIETY'. Similar signboards, albeit lesser in number, were put up for poultry and piggery societies, giving the required visibility and publicity to the programme.

The impressive progress we were making, particularly in setting up dairy cooperatives, received government recognition. One early morning, well before office hours, I received a telephone call from

Sarla Grewal, then Development Commissioner and who later became Principal Secretary to Prime Minister Rajiv Gandhi. As I answered the call, came her rhetorical question in Punjabi, 'Why can't we set up a cooperative milk plant in Hoshiarpur like in Gujarat?' I was certainly taken aback by this early morning call and my instinctive response was that we could. Whereupon she suggested I go to Anand where Amul is located and study that model for replication in Hoshiarpur. I spent a week in Anand, visiting milk cooperatives, run mainly by women, and studied the milk collection system and the processing. I noted two interesting differences between Gujarat and Punjab. First, in Gujarat it was entirely cow milk whereas in Punjab buffaloes were the main source. Second, Gujaratis were not great milk drinkers so they sold almost their entire produce, whereas a Punjabi was a copious milk-drinker, and so to generate surplus milk for sale, high yielding cattle would be imperative to make the programme successful.

In the following months, work on establishing more dairy cooperatives was accelerated. The Hoshiarpur District Cooperative Milk Producers Union was registered. Simultaneously, work was initiated on the project to set up two milk chilling plants, one in Dasuya and the second in Garhshankar, to support the cooperative milk plant in Hoshiarpur. The plan was to establish a milk plant with a capacity of 50,000 litres. The estimated cost of the project was Rs 1.15 crore. The state government contributed Rs15 lakh as subsidy from the MFAL Agency and the balance Rs 1 crore was loaned by the National Cooperative Development Corporation (NCDC) to the milk union. Negotiations were carried with two reputed, competing dairy plant manufacturers, Vulcan Laval and Larsen and Toubro. Both companies invited me to visit their manufacturing facilities as well as those of their principals overseas. My response was that we could dispense with that and they should deduct the related marketing costs from their quoted prices. The architectural plan and its technical aspects was another huge challenge but one learnt on the job.

We had an emissary from Dr Verghese Kurien, the man behind White Revolution and Anand in Gujarat, ostensibly to partner us in this venture but, more realistically, to take over the project. We were, however, determined to take the independent and pioneering path. In less than two years, the milk plant was constructed and ready to be commissioned. We had been able to complete the project not only before the target date but also with a saving of about 10 per cent of the estimated cost. When Chief Minister Giani Zail Singh inaugurated the plant, the project included two milk chilling plants which were also functional and about 100 village level dairy cooperative societies had become registered members of the cooperative milk plant. What was also very significant was that this was the first big industry to be set up in Hoshiarpur. A few years later, the plant underwent expansion and doubled its capacity, thereby further testifying to its success. From the initial about 100 village level milk cooperative societies forming the union, it has expanded to over 300 societies and currently the total enrolled membership of the union is nearly 25,000 with around 7,000 female members.

While going through the experience of setting up a milk plant, I observed with interest the milk plant being simultaneously set up in Ludhiana by the Punjab Dairy Development Corporation, the specialised government agency for dairy development in the state. Construction work on this plant of the same capacity of 50,000 litres had started a year before the Hoshiarpur project but it was completed almost two years later. The architectural design was indeed far more impressive as the emphasis appeared to be more on its aesthetic appeal than what was functionally suitable. For example, while the spray dryer for producing milk powder installed was the flat bottom model, as we had in our plant, the building design was a huge tower which would normally be required for the conical shaped dryer. Thus, while we had saved on civil construction, unnecessary cost was incurred in the other project to make the plant building look more monumental and impressive. When the plant was finally completed and was inaugurated by no less than the Prime Minister, it was hailed as a very successful project. No questions were asked either how much time it took to complete the project or how much it cost. Unfortunately, that is generally common in government projects where time and cost are often overlooked as being of no consequence.

The Hoshiarpur milk plant project was personally a very exciting experience for me and a huge learning process, especially as I had no engineering background. To have had this opportunity and experience within the first few years of my career in the IAS was hugely satisfying, especially as I believe no other profession would have given me this kind of opportunity. Equally exhilarating was establishing the network of dairy cooperatives all over the district. At the outset, organising dairy cooperatives was a daunting task as we were dealing with not only the more enlightened and progressive farmers but also those holding less than one hectare of land and landless agricultural labourers. My support team of former block development officers was well experienced in playing an advocacy role in promoting development related government initiatives. My standing instructions to them were to remain in the field with specific targets in mind and to give me a weekly report on the progress achieved. Once the initial groundwork was done, I would visit the villages to reassure the potential beneficiaries on the essential features of the scheme, namely provision of bank loan with subsidy, procurement of high milk-yielding buffaloes and assured marketing of milk with payment on a daily basis.

I was now beginning to feel more settled and reconciled to having joined the IAS. In fact, through this experience I went through a kind of mental metamorphosis. I felt fully involved and committed to my work and increasingly enjoyed working in the villages amongst the poorer sections of the rural population. It was a matter of great satisfaction that one was actually making a difference in improving their lives. By providing supplementary sources of income to marginal farmers and agricultural labourers, it helped to improve their food security index. The earnestness of the target group could also be gauged from the fact that loan repayments were regular and without default. I could not think of any other profession where this was achievable so soon and on such a scale.

Gone was that feeling of longing for the metropolitan lifestyle. Initially, I would try to be back in Delhi at any given opportunity and looked forward to socialising with my old friends there. But as time went by, I became conscious that the conversation among my friends appeared more and more superficial, and in fact, at times I felt like an outsider. I thought, 'How much out of touch with reality are they.' And when I was back at my work sitting amidst the rural poor and the deprived, I could feel how much they depended on me to help them in meeting their very basic needs and to make their lives more dignified. At times, I would wonder how they would react if they knew that just the day before I was wining and dining in a world totally unknown to them. A thought would often come to me. Who was the real me?—the one in the five-star culture of Delhi or the one sitting in the backward villages? That is when the metamorphosis took place and my approach to life and work underwent a significant change and, in a sense, I was thereafter equally comfortable in either situation.

5

Innovative Approaches

Life is a series of natural and spontaneous changes.
Don't resist them—that only creates sorrow.
Let reality be reality. Let things flow naturally
forward in whatever way they like.

—Lao Tzu

I had been in Hoshiarpur for almost four years, so a change was due any time. I was posted as Director, Tourism and moved to Chandigarh. For the Punjab government, tourism development was still a low priority and the department's budget was meagre. In contrast, the Haryana government was giving high priority, especially to developing tourist resorts along the Grand Trunk Road from Delhi to Chandigarh. Haryana's tourism development benefited from the brilliant vision of S.K. Misra (Chappy Misra) and the authority vested in him as Principal Secretary to the Chief Minister, to translate his vision to reality. It was unfortunate that the Punjab government, despite its rich heritage of art and culture as well as heritage buildings of the former princely states, failed to appreciate the potential of tourism to create employment and diversify development. I visited some of the heritage buildings in Patiala and Kapurthala and was disappointed to see that they were in a state of total neglect. Precious artefacts of immense value were stored in buildings declared unsafe. The fabulous collection of medals of Maharaja Bhupinder Singh of Patiala is the largest and the rarest in the world but they were stored in an old dilapidated building with minimal security. There was not even a proper inventory of the medals. I could visualise the task ahead and the problems one would encounter in getting the government to accord higher priority to archaeology and tourism development.

Before I could really settle in to my new responsibility, the unexpected happened. I was posted to Delhi as Administrator of the Punjab Pavilion for the 1974 India International Trade Fair (IITF). I never really understood why I was given this assignment. But a stint in Delhi was something I looked forward to. My office was adjoining the office of Resident Commissioner P.H. Vaishnav, a very popular officer belonging to the 1956 batch, at Punjab Bhawan. He belonged to Gujarat and was married to a Punjabi. He spoke faultless Punjabi and had totally identified himself with the Punjabi culture. He was widely respected in the Punjab cadre as a very outspoken and fearless officer. Perhaps, that led to his undoing and he was posted to Delhi in a relatively less important post. At our very first meeting, his friendly and informal demeanour broke down the barriers of seniority. I instantly developed great respect for him and we got along exceedingly well.

I got involved in planning the Punjab Pavilion with the guidance of Vaishnav. We commissioned the well-known artist, Satish Gujral, to make a mural for display at the entrance to the pavilion. But soon thereafter came the anti-climax. IITF was cancelled and all work relating thereto had to be stopped forthwith. I was asked to await my new posting orders which, for some inexplicable reason, took months. As Vaishnav's workload was quite light, he would call me to his office and we spent hours chatting over cups of tea.

One day, he told me that he had spoken to Chief Secretary R.S. Talwar, suggesting that a post of Additional Managing Director, Punjab State Industrial Development Corporation (PSIDC), be created and I be posted there, keeping in mind my successful experience in setting up the milk plant in Hoshiarpur. S.L. Kapur, Secretary, Industries, Punjab government, was also supportive, which I believed was more out of respect for Vaishnav's recommendation. Talwar was initially reluctant to link the creation of the post with my posting and so it took unduly long for the process to be completed.

While waiting for my next posting, I was given another unconventional assignment. Nobel laureate Har Gobind Khorana, who hailed from Punjab but settled in the USA, was to visit India. The Punjab government, laying claim to his ancestry, decided to treat him as a state guest and host his stay in Delhi. He was to stay at the Kapurthala House, which was the state guest house. As the guest house was in a dilapidated state, it was decided to refurbish it to make it suitable for the famous guest. This task of refurbishing was assigned to me, much to my surprise, especially since there was the office of the Chief Architect of Punjab or the Public Works Department which could have undertaken this work. But the Punjab government in its wisdom decided that I should do it. I went ahead to complete this assignment before the state guest arrived. Fortunately, the refurbishment was well appreciated. At a more personal level, in the few months I was idling in Delhi, I became a member of the Delhi

Golf Club, a much sought-after membership. Eventually, the post of Additional Managing Director was created and I received my posting orders towards the end 1974.

I approached my new assignment at the PSIDC with considerable excitement and enthusiasm, having enjoyed the experience of setting up the milk plant project. The Corporation had acquired a reputation of being a dynamic organisation. Further, in view of the considerable need for more industrial development, the Punjab government gave priority to promoting industrialization in the state. The Managing Director was A.S. Chatha of the 1963 batch, reputedly very dynamic and politically equally astute. Kapur was the Chairman of the PSIDC Board. In my first meeting with Chatha, I got an overview of the work of the PSIDC. I was impressed by Chatha's remarkable grasp of details, both technical and financial, regarding each project under implementation. The PSIDC's mission was clear: to address and fulfil the imperative need to diversify the economy of Punjab through industrial development, especially as agricultural land holdings were small and prospects for future growth on a sustained basis were limited. The PSIDC was mandated to promote industrial joint ventures with the private sector and thereby attract more investment and generate greater employment opportunities in the state. The flagship project at that time was Punjab Tractors Ltd., manufacturing the Swaraj tractors. There were projects on the anvil in various sectors, such as agro-processing, including a brewery, chemicals, steel, etc.

Initially, I was given charge as Chairman of the Board of some of the smaller projects including one to manufacture wireless sets and another relating to chemical plants. We set up a company, Punjab Wireless Ltd, for the wireless sets project with a group of young, budding technicians interested in developing prototypes of wireless sets for non-military use. We provided them a half-built facility not being used by another PSIDC venture, Punjab Chemi-Plants (P) Ltd, to carry out their work and eventually they developed the prototype and went into commercial production of wireless handsets under the name PUNWIRE. Among the major clients were government agencies handling airports, security, law and order, etc. Punjab Chemi-Plants was set up to manufacture plant and machinery for chemicals but as the demand increased for Indian companies to take up civil construction projects in the Middle East, it diversified taking up large civil construction projects such as housing colonies in Kuwait.

During one of the review meetings with Chief Minister Giani Zail Singh, we gave an undertaking to have him lay the foundation stone of one project a month for a full year. This meant 12 projects ready with a tie-up with a private sector partner, site selection as well as assured technical and financial arrangements. It was a matter of great satisfaction that we lived up to our commitment. In due course, I had realised that to work effectively in an organisation like the PSIDC, one had to think out of the box and not be tied down to file work alone, in order to be as efficient and competitive as the private sector. This was perhaps the biggest challenge, to be businesslike and be ready to take commercial risks while working in a government organisation that is typically ridden with bureaucratic rules and procedures curbing efficiency and enterprise. There were indeed situations when one had to take initiatives, disregarding conventional bureaucratic norms and be more pragmatic. Dealing with such situations was the highlight of my tenure in the PSIDC and is elaborated here.

In order to diversify industrial development in the state, we decided to give special attention to the development of electronics industry in the state. This programme was under my charge. When we submitted the first electronics related joint venture proposal to the Central government for approving import of technology, it was referred to the Electronics Commission, headed by Ashok Parthasarathi, for its consideration. The Electronics Commission advised that as the technology was available with Bharat Electronics, a public sector undertaking in Bangalore, there was no need to import it. We were, therefore, advised to approach Bharat Electronics for transfer of technology. However, Bharat Electronics was reluctant to share the technology with us. In their view, as they were able to meet the entire demand in the country, there was no need to set up any additional capacity. Hence, we were left in a peculiar predicament where Bharat Electronics declined to share the technology and the Electronics Commission was neither willing to intervene on our behalf nor was it ready to change its earlier stand against import of technology.

During my earlier visits to Bharat Electronics, I had met some of the senior heads of divisions dealing with the manufacture of different electronic components. Faced with this impasse, I visited Bangalore again and contacted the heads of three different divisions to meet me at Ashok Hotel. I explained to them that the Punjab government was giving high priority to diversify the state's economy by promoting industrialization and that impressive progress had been made in promoting joint ventures in agro-processing, chemicals, etc. and currently a major focus was on developing the electronics industry. I invited them to Punjab with the allurement that we would appoint each of them as managing director of enterprises to manufacture electronic components. They were visibly interested in the prospect of promoting their professional career from employees to entrepreneurs. The terms offered were also attractive enough for them to accept the offer and move to Punjab. That is how we started the development of electronics industries in Punjab. As expected, the management of

Bharat Electronics was livid and banned our entry to their facility in future. The Electronics Commission intervened after receiving a complaint from Bharat Electronics. We responded with the explanation that under the restrictive policy on import of technology and Bharat Electronics wanting to monopolise production, we were left with no choice but to hire the experts. Fortunately, the policy on import of electronics technology progressively became more liberal and we did not have to resort to such measures for other electronics projects.

One such project requiring technology import was the manufacture of ceramic capacitors. We had narrowed down to AVX Inc. in Myrtle Beach, South Carolina, USA. I travelled to the US, stopping in Europe for a few days in connection with another project, to finalise the collaboration. As I arrived in New York, I called Dick Rosen, vice-president, with whom I was to meet and sign the agreement, just to inform him that I had arrived in New York en route to Myrtle Beach. Expecting some words of welcome, I was taken aback when Rosen expressed surprise that I had come. Apparently, another Indian party was also in touch with AVX, seeking technical collaboration and had signed an agreement with AVX just a few days before. Thereupon, Rosen had sent a telex to us calling off our meeting, as they could not sign with another Indian party. The telex perhaps arrived during my stopover in Europe but was never communicated to me.

I told Rosen that since I had come to the US solely for this purpose, we could at least meet without any commitment. 'What will we discuss?' he asked. My response was, 'I believe Myrtle Beach is famous for golf, so if you play golf, we could meet over a round of golf and discuss the weather.' With a touch of amusement, Rosen agreed and suggested that since the following Monday was 'Yiddish Kipper' and a holiday, I could contact him on Tuesday. I contacted him as agreed and we fixed a round of golf that afternoon. He was just a beginner and it was more of a social outing over nine holes. Our conversation was essentially getting acquainted with each other and I was careful not to even allude to the project. When parting after golf, Rosen invited me to a cookout he was having at his home that evening which I immediately accepted. As I arrived at his home, he introduced me to his wife remarking that I had 'tickled his funny bone' as I had kept my word and not said anything about the project.

At the end of the evening, Rosen asked me to meet him at his office the next morning. When we met, he explained his predicament as he had already signed with the other party from Mumbai. I noted that the other party was a consultancy firm that would be looking to find a client to set up the project. I explained to Rosen that the agreement would need to be approved by the Government of India and we, as a state organisation, would have a much better chance of getting the approval than a broker of their technology. I, therefore, suggested that we sign an agreement on the same terms and conditions and leave it open for AVX to collaborate with whichever party could get the government approval. Rosen was convinced that it was reasonable and so we signed the agreement. A few months later, we had got approval from the Central government and a joint venture was set up in Mohali, Punjab. Rosen came to the foundation stone laying ceremony of our joint venture, with a custom-made golf set as a gift.

In the course of setting up the project with AVX Inc., I had to visit Myrtle Beach a few times. It is not just a golfer's paradise but also a very popular seaside resort among the Americans, offering tennis and water sports. The local population was about 12,000 but over a long weekend like the Labour Day weekend, when I happened to be there, the population would swell with holiday-makers to over two hundred thousand. And the very next day, the streets would again be deserted, 'vacancy' signs would be up and it would revert to being a quiet sleepy town. On my first visit, I visited a store called 'Cheap Joey', to buy a pair of jeans for my brother, Ricky (Rakesh). The owner was a huge portly figure with a typical southern drawl. The usual questions were: 'Where are you from? How come you speak English so well?', etc. But this drew us into an interesting conversation. He suddenly mentioned Sai Baba and asked me about him. Apparently, the biggest real estate business woman in Myrtle Beach was a follower of Sai Baba of Puttaparthi and held a congregation every Thursday which attracted a sizable section of the local population. I shared whatever I knew about Sai Baba adding a casual suggestion that if there was so much interest in Sai Baba, he could have a small section in his shop for Indian clothes, trinkets, etc. He smiled and nodded his head. When I revisited the shop about a year later, the shop had been completely transformed to an Indian shop and he was doing roaring business. He greeted me with a big hug and called his wife and daughter to come to the shop to meet 'my Indian friend'.

Sometimes, the most unexpected things happen which impact one's life. On another trip to the US to negotiate technical collaboration with Repco in Orlando, Florida for manufacturing electronic resistors, I arrived over the weekend and checked into the Holiday Inn. I was to meet the vice-president and his wife that evening for an informal dinner. I decided to take a stroll to get a feel of the place that afternoon. As I walked down a street, I passed a huge store selling glassware. I saw a small door which I opened and walked in. As I walked around the store, I suddenly realised that there was no one there. And then it dawned on me that being a weekend, the store was actually closed and the owner must have forgotten to lock that door. I rushed out of the store before I could be accused of breaking in. That evening over dinner, I related this potentially horrific incident to my hosts. The store owner happened to be their friend so they called him. He called back admitting he had forgotten to lock the side entrance and conveyed his gratitude to me. My host's wife jocularly remarked that he should have backed his gratitude with a gift. I told her that I was just relieved to have not got into an embarrassing situation, especially being a government official in a foreign country. Sunday was well spent with a visit to Disney World, a treat for everyone regardless of age. Unfortunately, the collaboration with Repco did not fructify.

I had been in the PSIDC for about two years when the Chief Secretary informed me that the Punjab Congress was going to host a party session in Kamagata Maru Nagar, near Chandigarh, and Chief Minister Giani Zail Singh wanted the government to put up an exhibition showcasing Punjab's development. He wanted the exhibition to be very impressive as important Congress leaders from all over the country, including Prime Minister Indira Gandhi, would be attending. This assignment was given to me as additional charge. The Congress session was to be held by December-end, 1975 that is, I had time of about six weeks only. I was filled with trepidation as it seemed an almost impossible task with the attendant risk to one's reputation. The only relieving factor was that I still retained my job in the PSIDC as I was in the midst of several project initiatives. I was again curious as to why the assignment was not given to a more appropriate department like that of the Chief Architect. Maybe it was because I had earlier been assigned as Administrator, Punjab Pavilion, and though the IITF had been cancelled, it might have been felt that I had acquired some experience, at least in planning, if not in actual execution.

Soon, a meeting was held by S.L. Kapur, Secretary Industries, to work out the budget and details of the exhibition. I was given a free hand as far as the conceptual aspects were concerned and a provisional budget was indicated. I expressed my reservations that given the limited time available, it would be impossible to complete the project in time if we were to follow the normal government procedures and norms for inviting tenders before selecting the design and construction contractors. Fortunately, this issue was well appreciated and I was given the freedom to dispense with normal procedures and shorten the process wherever required.

Within a few days, I engaged an architect who was reputed, experienced and innovative in both designing and execution. He suggested a contractor who had worked with him in various projects so he could testify to his competence and reliability. I accepted his recommendation as it was important to have a team with mutual confidence and compatibility. I emphasised to the team that the Chief Minister was categorical that the Punjab exhibition should be extraordinary in design and impressive in content considering that it would be visited by Prime Minister Indira Gandhi and important Congress leaders. However, we had to also keep in mind the limited time available to complete the project. Hence, we planned a design which would enable off-site work to be carried out simultaneously with construction at the site.

Consequently, the prefabricated structure was built offsite while the foundation was being constructed onsite. It was also necessary that the structure should not be permanent as it would have to be dismantled soon after the session was over. The prefabricated structure of steel pipes was tubular in shape and the roofing was made of heavy polyethylene with colourful motifs, typical to Punjab's folk art. Most importantly, this would not only be more cost effective and would enable us to have a large area for exhibits but most of the building material used could be recycled. As far as exhibits were concerned, we agreed to use, as far as possible, existing material with emphasis on photographic depiction of various government development schemes. The Haryana government also decided to set up a pavilion at a nearby site which turned out to be the common brick and mortar structure.

The execution work was taken up on a round-the-clock basis. Often I would take packed dinner from home for the supervisors as a token of my appreciation for the extraordinary effort on their part—a gesture that was duly appreciated. The Public Information Department was assisting in preparing the photo exhibits. Some heavy machinery like the Swaraj tractor and agriculture machinery was being readied to be displayed in the open areas around the pavilion. However, at the site just the work on the foundation was visible.

A team of Congress leaders came occasionally to check the progress and expressed shock at what appeared to them to be an ensuing disaster. Their infuriation was even greater when they saw the Haryana pavilion structure of brick and mortar was at almost completion stage. They threatened me that while I might not be worried about the looming disaster, I should realise that my career was at stake. Frankly, it was a period of extreme tension. Several questions haunted me: What if the pavilion is not ready on time? What if this untested prefabricated steel structure was not strong enough to withstand the weight of the heavy polyethylene roofing? These were some of the many nightmarish thoughts passing through my mind. Although the architect assured me otherwise, these fears persisted.

Once the work shifted to the site and the steel structure was built, the pavilion started taking shape. A week before the deadline, the full structure was in place and we proceeded with the placement of the exhibits. The night before the start of the Congress session, the pavilion was completed and it presented, to quote, 'a breathtaking view'. At night the polyethylene roof glowed with colourful motifs and the wind tunnels between each arch, provided passage for the wind, and, which at the same time, inflated the roof. It was something very imaginative and unique, something not seen before. The spectacular glow of the pavilion could be seen from various parts of Chandigarh, attracting a large number of curious visitors.

The exhibition presented a historical perspective of Punjab's development through dramatic photographs and visuals. Sanjay and Maneka Gandhi were among the first to visit the exhibition. Later Prime Minister Indira Gandhi, accompanied by Chief Minister Zail Singh, visited and I personally guided them through the exhibition. The Prime Minister spent considerable time and evinced keen interest in various aspects of Punjab's development. Importantly, considerable appreciation was expressed, even by the earlier naysayers, for the unique concept and aesthetic display. If I were to draw a present-day parallel in terms of the external design and concept, it is like the tubular structure of the Suvarnabhumi International Airport in Bangkok, Thailand, which incidentally came up about 20 years later.

After the two-day Congress session was over, things were coming back to near normalcy and I was back full-time to my work in the PSIDC. The Department of Public Information had taken charge of the pavilion and its dismantling. However, a small whispering campaign had started questioning the cost and lack of accountability. It was reportedly initiated by the Chief Architect, who was piqued at having been ignored for this prestigious assignment and as far as I could gather, with support from just one sympathetic IAS officer. His motive remains a mystery to me as I had never worked with him. It was perhaps out of a sense of frustration of having been kept out of the mainstream of the government work. Kapur heard of this whispering campaign and he brought it to the attention of the Chief Minister. One afternoon I was called to Giani Zail Singh's residence and he complimented me for having successfully undertaken the assignment, especially against heavy odds and said that I should not be bothered by what some people were saying. I went away feeling reassured and soon the whispers also died down as there were no takers. This assignment, however, did take its toll. A few days after it was over and all the pent up tension was abating, I suddenly felt I was collapsing. The doctor diagnosed the condition as hypertension and put me on medication to control high blood pressure. I continue to be on this medication.

Punjab Breweries Ltd was a joint venture with Oberoi Hotels. The Managing Director of the company had left, so I was given temporary charge till a new person was appointed. At that time, efforts were underway to expand the market for its 'Charger' brand of beer and two target areas identified for immediate attention were Shillong in the North East and Mumbai. I first visited Shillong to study the market there. The main consumers seemed to be college students, and a visit to popular bars showed a majority of them were recipients of scholarships which explained their purchasing power for beer! It was a worrisome revelation and so ended our further marketing efforts there.

In Mumbai, Oberoi Hotels organised a promotional event at their hotel where a sales pitch was to be made. I arrived in Mumbai the day before the event and as I checked in, I was informed that I was on the VIP floor. Later that day when I returned to the hotel, I was accosted by a young, attractive lady, who seemed somewhat upset. She was standing near my room and then she turned to me and said to me accusingly: 'You smoke hash?' I was startled by this accusation and that too on the VIP floor! I denied vehemently but agreed with her there was a strange smell pervading the corridor. She was staying just two rooms away and was also a VIP guest. We walked down the corridor to figure out where the smell was coming from. It seemed to be coming from a room at the end of the corridor, which happened to be occupied by a member of the Oberoi family.

The promotional event was a great success with an impressive turnout and everyone seemed to be enjoying the beer. There were a few familiar faces I had not met for years. In the course of that evening, I was introduced to the young lady I had encountered the day before. She was with her mother, both looking strikingly elegant. I was told that they were the family of our Ambassador to Iraq, Romesh Bhandari. Being very good friends of the Oberoi family, they were temporarily staying in the hotel as their apartment was being furnished. How would I have known then that one day this young, attractive and elegant lady, Madhu, would become my wife! Next day I returned to Chandigarh and back to work.

A few weeks later, I happened to be in Delhi and was spending an evening with a couple who were good old friends. In the course of our conversation, I told them about my interesting encounter in Mumbai. They happened to know the family well and remarked that Madhu was going to be in Delhi in a few days and whether I would like to meet her again. I thought why not and so we agreed to meet again when she was in Delhi. A few days later when I was introduced to Madhu, I remarked that we had already met. She looked uncertain much to my puzzlement. Anyway, it turned out be a very pleasant evening and I told Madhu that I was going to be in Mumbai again on work in a few weeks and would look forward to meeting her. We did meet again when I was back in Mumbai but she always brought along a few friends. Our conversation was mostly exchanging jokes as she seemed more at ease at that.

Nevertheless, I started thinking, 'Is she the one?' One evening after a dinner with Madhu and her mother at the Oberoi Hotel, I offered to drop them at their apartment on Malabar Hill. When we reached there, I joined them for a cup of coffee. While Madhu made the coffee, I chatted with her mother. Later when I was alone with Madhu, I spontaneously proposed to her. She was silent for a while, thinking and scratching her chin and then said, 'I think so'. I took that as a yes and we broke it to her mother. Next morning, I called my mother and told her. She was understandably excited and relieved as both my younger brothers had already got married and I was causing her immense worry about my bachelorhood. That evening, after having proposed to Madhu, I had offered to accompany her to Crawford Market the next day where she was going to buy vegetables to be sent to Baghdad. At the market, I was a silent witness to her vegetable shopping. Madhu was buying vegetables without checking prices and the gleeful shopkeeper seemed to be having a field day. He was making her buy some strange looking vegetables which, on my asking, she was unable to identify. I thought to myself with amusement as to how was she going to manage that on my salary. I left Mumbai later that day on my way back feeling very happy with life and mesmerised with thoughts of Madhu.

A few months later, I had to go to Germany and I planned to stop over on my return journey in Baghdad to meet my future father-in-law for the first time. I had to go to Germany along with our private sector partner to negotiate the purchase of shoe manufacturing machinery from a company in Pirmasens, a German town famous for leather industry and manufacture of shoes. We stayed at a nearby village in a boutique hotel which was formerly the mansion of the owner of a historical brewery nearby. To my utter delight the owner was a connoisseur of Indian teas and had a stock of the finest teas including my favourite brand, Lopchu Orange Pekoe. He was also very particular that tea must be brewed correctly and served properly, serving in brown clay teapots for morning tea and black clay teapots for breakfast. We were there for about 10 days. The entire day was spent in negotiations in the company's office followed by an evening across the border to France to dine in restaurants, serving the choicest French cuisine. This was a memorable trip, not least for the perfect tea service! If there was anything I found wanting during all my travels, it was the availability of good tea, for tea bags were poor substitutes. I inherited this passion for good tea from my parents. To them, tea was not just a beverage, it was a cultural thing. I recall even during my school days when we went out on 'town leave', I would often go by myself to Davicos, a stylish restaurant from the British days, serving Lopchu tea and delicious pineapple cakes. The typical Punjabi likes tea boiled with milk and sugar and, often with spices in it, served in a glass, what I call 'tea-curry'. Because of my notoriety for being a very finicky tea drinker, my friends would dread the thought that I might drop in at tea time. Some actually kept a tea set and even a packet of Lopchu tea ready in case I did.

En route from Germany, I stopped over, as planned, in Baghdad to meet Ambassador Bhandari. Madhu, her mother and younger brother Sidharth were also there. Her elder brother Kavi was in Mumbai and I had already met him there. The warmth of the welcome extended by Madhu's father was both disarming and reassuring and I felt comfortable from the very start. It was early evening and my reputation as a fastidious tea drinker had already preceded me. Tea was served in great style and everyone's eyes were on me as I took my first sip. The tea was the antithesis of good flavoured steaming hot beverage. I tried to look as normal as possible but Madhu detected a sign of a grimace. She later explained to me that her family were not ardent tea drinkers and so the tea there was what was easily available. Interestingly, each time tea was served, the crockery looked better but not much could be done about the quality of tea. Anyway, that was unimportant and it became a matter of great amusement for all of us. The welcome party that evening was thoroughly enjoyable, meeting many interesting people, including some senior members of the Iraqi government. It was very obvious that Madhu's father was extremely popular among a cross-section of the very distinguished society of Baghdad. I left after a couple of days later carrying very happy memories and looking forward to getting married to Madhu.

6

Mixed Blessings

I will not follow where the path may lead,
but I will go where there is no path,
and I will leave a trail.

—Muriel Strode

Soon after my return to Chandigarh, the news of my approaching marriage spread across my social circle as well as, in a limited way, among colleagues in the government. The wedding was being planned for early 1977, i.e. just a few months away, so till then I was back to normal life and work. A few weeks later, Madhu called me asking me to accompany her and her mother to Bangkok to meet Her Majesty the Queen of Thailand. I was completely taken by surprise by this very unusual request. As I was to understand later, Madhu's father had been Ambassador to Thailand in the early 1970s and during his four-year tenure, they had become very good friends of King Bhumibol Adulyadej and Queen Sirikit. Madhu's father met the King quite frequently and I believe, occasionally they would attend discourses in Buddhism conducted by a common teacher who later became the Supreme Patriarch of Thailand. Madhu's mother Kumudesh Bhandari also belongs to a royal family—she is the daughter of Maharaja Bhupinder Singh of Patiala. This perhaps also contributed to strengthening the bond between her and the Queen. When the eldest daughter of Their Majesties Princess Ubolratana married an American in 1972 against all royal protocol, they were extremely upset and the Princess was stripped of all royal titles and ostracized. At that time, the Queen had expressed her dismay and cautioned Madhu's mother. Apparently Madhu's mother responded by saying that before Madhu got married, she would get the Queen's endorsement. Hence, the visit to Bangkok and tea with the Queen!

This was my first visit to Bangkok, not knowing then that I would visit this city very frequently and, eventually, it would become our second home. We stayed at Thanpuying Lursakdi's house whose family is among the most highly reputed and respected in Thailand. They, too, were very close friends, more like an extended family from the time Madhu's father was Ambassador to Thailand. She belonged to the renowned Nai Lert family of Thailand and thus had very close links to the royal family. The family owned the largest bus transport service in Bangkok till it was nationalized in the early 1970s. Quite befittingly, Lursakdi became the Transport Minister, which was her first foray into politics. She remained minister till the government of Prime Minister Thanin K. was overthrown in a military coup. Her husband, who we called Uncle Binich, a portly and jovial figure, was immersed in the world of art and was curator of the national museum, totally unrelated to the family's businesses. After the coup, the family converted part of their huge estate into a hotel, initially with the Hilton group. Their daughters, Peg and Pag, became very good friends of Madhu and continue to be among our closest friends in Bangkok. When the coup took place, they were sent for safe custody to the Indian Ambassador's residence; such was the closeness between the two families. Madhu and Pag were together in a finishing school Villa Brillantmont in Lausanne, Switzerland. Whenever the Queen visited Switzerland, she would call them and mentor them on how to conduct themselves while living in a foreign country. Pag and her husband Dang, whose family owned the largest spinning plant in Asia, continued to be among our closest friends when we relocated to Bangkok many years later.

The tea session with the Queen was extremely pleasant in spite of all the heavy protocol. Her elegance and charm were disarming and she was very soft-spoken, speaking in almost loud whispers. Reflecting back, I was not at all accustomed to the formal protocol and totally unaware how much Their Majesties were revered by the people of Thailand, and so my conversation and demeanour was perhaps too informal. The Queen expressed her desire to send her daughter Princess Maha Chakri to India to study Sanskrit and asked whether we could be her local guardians which we readily accepted. It was indicative of the mutual closeness and confidence that existed between the two families. However, Princess Maha Chakri never came to India to study Sanskrit. Instead, a Sanskrit teacher went from India to teach her. Many years later, when I happened to receive Princess Maha Chakri during her visit to the United Nations, I reminded her of this conversation. She said that she was still very much involved in the study of Sanskrit and was sponsoring two scholarships a year for learning Sanskrit in India.

During this visit, I also met some friends of Madhu's family who were of Indian origin. Chimanbhai Shah, the head of a highly successful commodity trading company, GP Group. He was an excellent host and we spent some very wonderful evenings together. His son, Kirit, would in time build a business empire of unimaginable proportions. He and his wife Anju would later become good friends of ours in Bangkok. Then there was Vashi Purswani whose tailoring shop, Martin Tailors, was famous for stitching safari suits that were very much in fashion then. He has since diversified impressively and ranks among the more prominent business leaders in the Indian diaspora. He and his wife Roop and their family, too, would, in course of time, be among our closest friends. Quite clearly, if one were to see Indian enterprise flourish, Thailand was the country. The Birla group had already established itself with a number of successful enterprises showcasing Indian technology and entrepreneurship.

In Chandigarh, life became even busier between my work and preparing for the wedding which was fixed for 7 February, 1977, in Delhi. I was the last among all my school friends to get married and that too by a significant gap. A few were already on their second round! Hence, it became an event eagerly awaited and was well attended by friends in addition to family and relatives. Madhu got to know that Amitabh Bachchan was in Delhi and, knowing my old association with him, insisted that I invite him to attend at least one of the pre-wedding functions, if not the wedding. My association with Amitabh goes back to our college days and years later, renewing contact with him when he was working in Kolkata. I sent him a message and he was there at one of the pre-wedding parties in Oberoi Hotel, where he was staying. Punjab Chief Minister Zail Singh came to the wedding and very graciously spent considerable time with my family.

There was similarly a large gathering of well-known personalities and celebrities on Madhu's side. The *barat* was received in the traditional

Patiala style and ceremonies conducted with all the solemnity and traditions of an Indian wedding. Madhu's face was totally covered, as is the custom, and so at the *jaimala* (a wedding ritual) when the bride and groom garland each other, I whispered, 'Is that you?' and she gave a reassuring nod. Some of my old school friends, particularly Mukhi and Sukhi, tried to interject some Bollywood songs and that too in the most unmusical manner, during the actual wedding ceremony, undeterred by the stern looks they got from the bride's side. Our two-week honeymoon was spent mainly in Goa, Kerala and few other places in the South, as Madhu, having spent most of her life in foreign countries, had never visited South India.

Back in Chandigarh, Madhu settled in easily and within a short time. My friend Sunny Jind had given me his house as it was lying vacant and he was worried that his estranged wife would try to grab it. It was a large five-bedroom house built over an acre of land in Sector 9, a prime location in Chandigarh. The huge garden was full of flowers and fruit trees, and offered enough space for the four poodles that Madhu had brought along, to run around. Our social life also got into full gear with both friends and colleagues in the government. I had an excellent cook, so my parties were known for the cuisine. The only difference was, as one senior lady officer remarked, earlier all the guests were in the air-conditioned room but now that privilege had been given to the dogs!

I was back to my work in the PSIDC. One morning I received a telephone call from the Ministry of External Affairs (MEA) which took me completely by surprise. The call was to enquire whether the PSIDC would be interested in participating in a Tuna fish canning project in the Maldives. I jocularly remarked that as far as I could see from my office window, there was no Tuna fish in Punjab, so why would we be interested. The MEA indicated that the project to be set up in the Maldives had encountered some unexpected problems in implementation, which they wanted to discuss with us. I was understandably curious why the MEA had chosen to contact us as the PSIDC's mandate was essentially to promote industry in Punjab and undertaking projects in foreign countries was never envisaged.

Hence, my preliminary question at the meeting was why the PSIDC was being approached for the project in the Maldives. The MEA explained that the Indian government had gifted a Tuna fish canning plant to the Maldives as a token of friendship and, under the agreement, the civil construction and erection of the plant was to be done by the Maldives government. However, after the plant and machinery were delivered at the site in Felivaru Island, the Maldives government expressed its inability to execute its part of the agreement and so had requested the Indian government to find an Indian party that could undertake completion of the project. The MEA had approached several private sector companies but they all declined because there was no clarity on policy and laws in the Maldives relating to security of foreign investment and repatriation of profits.

The MEA then decided to look for some state-run organisation to bail it out from any potential embarrassment. The PSIDC's reputation as a dynamic organisation had prompted the MEA to approach us. I said the concerns of the private sector were valid and would be of relevance to us as well. The Ministry, not being fully informed on these matters, urged that without committing ourselves, we meet with the Maldives government and seek all required clarifications and assurances. The MEA's underlying fear was that if the project remained unimplemented, the leverage and goodwill sought to be achieved would be nullified and the friendly gesture might become counterproductive.

It was, therefore, understandable that the Ministry was determined to at least demonstrate to the Maldives government that it had made an earnest attempt to respond positively to their request and bail them out of a difficult situation. The PSIDC accordingly agreed to meet with the Maldives government and I was asked to undertake the mission.

There was no direct flight to the Maldives and one had to go from Colombo, Sri Lanka. I travelled from Trivandrum to Colombo and then on to Hulhule Island where the airport is located. As this was a totally unexpected and my first trip to the Maldives, I was looking forward to being in what was emerging as a very popular tourist destination. Approaching the Maldives one got a breathtaking view of the atolls, forming a pattern of a deep green core, encircled by white sand, and then by turquoise colour water and again a white ring where the sea breaks into the coral reef. At the airport I was received by the Indian High Commissioner to Sri Lanka, Gurbachan Singh, a very experienced diplomat who perhaps was on his last posting before retirement and was also accredited to the Maldives. He had come to the Maldives especially for this purpose and accompanying him was our Consul General in the Maldives. India was the only country to have a consulate in Male and the only other foreign institution there was Habib Bank of Pakistan.

The welcome was warm but I sensed an undercurrent of embarrassment. Gurbachan Singh soon spoke out and said that when the Consul General had approached the Maldives government to make my appointments, he was informed that the government had already signed an agreement with the Japanese to set up the plant in Felivaru. The Japanese had struck a deal to complete the project and in addition to build a jetty in return for getting Tuna fishing rights in the Maldives territorial waters. This agreement had been signed when a Japanese delegation had visited Male just a few days before and so, quite understandably, the Maldives government saw no purpose in meeting with us. The only minister, who was willing to meet and had given an appointment, was the Minister of Tourism. I wondered how on an island as small as Male, a Japanese delegation could arrive and sign an agreement, unknown to the Indian Consul General, but maintained a discreet silence.

As the next flight back was only five days later, I had to perforce stay in Male. As Male was just the capital, it had no proper facilities for foreign guests such as hotels, restaurants, etc. I had to stay in a rather modest accommodation. Passing time was a huge problem. One could walk from one end of Male to the other in less than an hour. It would have taken even less time had there been a paved road throughout. Gurbachan Singh had stayed at one of the tourist resort islands, and as there was no real official work to be conducted, he left for Colombo a day later. The meeting with the Minister of Tourism was cordial and we went through the motions of discussing the Maldives potential for tourism but with no real intent, at least from my side. The only positive outcome was his invite to me to visit one of the tourist resorts, which I accepted willingly. A day's trip was organised to Helengeli Island. I was amazed at the tourism facilities there and also felt even more disappointed about my forced stay at Male. The day was spent on the beach and snorkelling to see the most fascinating coral reefs. Perhaps in an attempt to appease me, the Consul General told me that I had been saved from undertaking a boat trip of about seven hours across the choppy sea to Felivaru, the site of the project. His explanation was not convincing, and I returned home after a futile trip. The Indian government had to reconcile to just gifting the plant and machinery to the Maldives.

In addition to promoting industrial joint ventures, the PSIDC was also taking initiatives to develop entrepreneurship in the state. Punjab Wireless was one example where a group of young engineers was assisted to set up a manufacturing unit which successfully went into commercial production of PUNWIRE wireless sets.

In another case, the brother duo, Mukhinder Singh and Sukhinder Singh—my old school friends, Mukhi and Sukhi who sang Bollywood songs at my wedding, and former fighter pilots in the Indian Air Force—collaborated as private sector partners with the PSIDC to set up a paper manufacturing plant in Mukerian, Hoshiarpur district. At that time, the PSIDC was according priority to agro-processing projects and had on the anvil a project for converting grass into paper. In Hoshiarpur district, there was abundance of 'babbar grass' which helped in determining the location of the project in Mukerian. The plant and machinery was imported from Germany, and Sukhinder Singh, as Managing Director, successfully installed and managed the plant, Mukerian Papers Ltd. Subsequently, they decided to disinvest and Sukhi used that experience to undertake on his own a large food-processing venture in Punjab.

While in Chandigarh, I had another important responsibility, but unrelated to my official work. I had been elected president of the Old Cottonians Association, India. It is an association of old boys belonging to Bishop Cotton School, Shimla. The school being over a hundred years old, the association had a very large membership of Old Cottonians. There were differences between the association's relations with the school board, chaired by the Bishop of Amritsar. The effects of a dispute in the Amritsar Diocese had percolated to the school board, thereby disrupting its functioning. The association had two representatives on the board, one being the president. Bishop Joseph, who was holding temporary charge of the diocese, had been reluctant to have a meeting of the school board, citing a stay order from the Himachal Pradesh High Court. After I took over as president, I contacted Bishop Joseph to give me a copy of the stay order. As I had suspected, the stay order did not prevent the board from meeting and so, at my insistence, the Bishop was compelled to call a meeting of the board. The meeting was attended by my peer Anil Mehra (Dimpy), a renowned chartered accountant, and me. The Deputy Commissioner of Shimla was also on the board, who at that time happened to be an IAS officer, two years my junior. He was duly apprised of the problems we were facing and so was willing to support us. At the meeting we were able to get decisions to reconstitute the board, carry on an internal audit of accounts, review the quality of the teaching faculty and take cognizance of some alleged corruption in procurement of supplies.

In the course of the next few months, Dimpy and I had to make several trips to the school to undertake the follow-up work. As a chartered accountant, Dimpy was fully geared to undertake the internal audit. The board was reconstituted to include some more eminent members such as the Principal of St. Stephen's College, which was expected to also facilitate the admission of more Cottonians into that college. I interviewed all the teaching staff members and found several of them were below average and a few mismatched in terms of their qualifications and what they were teaching. The Senior Master, Advani, had been in the school during my time. In fact, he had in a way been a factor in my coming to the school. There were corruption charges against his son who had taken over various supplies to the school. I called the Senior Master and confronting him with the allegations advised him to resign citing personal reasons to save him from the ignominy of being dismissed after so many years of service to the school. He resigned a few days later. Headmaster Goldstein had aged and thus was unable to administer the school effectively. He, too, was advised to resign at the end of the year. In the meanwhile, we planned to look for someone with reputable credentials to replace him.

Unfortunately, during one of my overseas tours, Bishop Joseph recruited a replacement, Brig. Mukand, without any consultation with the board. When I protested, he assured me that it was just a stop-gap arrangement till we found a suitable replacement. Very disappointingly, the Bishop had lied and gradually this person got entrenched in connivance with him. He carried on as headmaster for several years, in fact till his passing away, and it was always a battle to prevent him from changing the character of the school and discarding its traditions. This unfortunate episode left a sense of disillusionment about the integrity of a bishop.

At the national level, the political situation was in an upheaval, after Prime Minister Indira Gandhi had declared an Emergency in 1975. She was advised to hold elections in 1977 to consolidate her power. This miscalculation led to her defeat and the Janata Party came into power with Morarji Desai as Prime Minister. In Punjab, too, there was a change. The Congress government, having completed its term, was defeated by the Akali Dal and Parkash Singh Badal became the Chief Minister. Normally, as a bureaucrat, one should feel insulated from such political changes but the unexpected can always happen.

Chief Secretary S.S. Puri called me and said that the Chief Minister had decided to launch an integrated rural development programme in Punjab and he had already requested the Prime Minister to inaugurate it in about two months' time. There was only the objective but no substance, hence the urgency to conceptualize a programme.

Apparently, in the Chief Secretary's consultations with senior colleagues, there was a general consensus that this task should be assigned to me. Perhaps my experience in Hoshiarpur had prompted their recommendation. I said that I was very happy working in the PSIDC so given a choice, I would prefer to continue there. The Chief Secretary said Development Commissioner K.S. Bains, under whose responsibility this programme was to be developed, had insisted that I should be given this assignment. (He was Deputy Commissioner in Amritsar when I underwent my district training and had undertaken field work.) The Chief Secretary quipped that the whole idea seemed 'very woolly-woolly' to him and so wished me luck!

In a few days, I was transferred and appointed to the newly created post of Additional Development Commissioner to conceptualise and implement the first integrated rural development programme in Punjab. I left the PSIDC reluctantly but at the same time with a sense of satisfaction over the work achieved and the experience gained. Also acknowledging the fact that in government service, transfers and postings were inevitable.

The Punjab Integrated Rural Development Programme was to be ready for inauguration by the Prime Minister in less than two months. Dr Kahlon from Punjab Agriculture University was deputed to assist me in conceptualizing the programme. The only guiding indication we got was that the inspiration to have such a programme came to the Chief Minister from E.F. Schumacher's book *Small is Beautiful*.

After brainstorming over various models for people-centred rural development, we narrowed down to a 'cluster of villages' approach. A spatial plan was prepared with clusters of five villages, one of which would be the 'focal point' village, in every development block. The 'focal point' village would become the centre for sourcing agricultural inputs like seeds, fertilizers, pesticides, etc. as well as have the infrastructure for support services like rural credit banks for short-term farm loans, agricultural marketing, veterinary hospitals, etc. As the selection of the 'focal point' village was of critical importance to ensure that it serves its cluster effectively, a criterion was laid out. For example, the connectivity of the 'focal point' village with the other four villages and the normal movement of people were important considerations. Thus, a cluster of five villages with a 'focal point' in each development block was formed as the first phase of the programme to demonstrate its efficacy. After tireless work and burning a lot of midnight oil, we conceptualized the programme and it received the Chief Minister's endorsement.

The next step was to make preparations on a war footing for the inauguration of the programme by Prime Minister Morarji Desai, just a few weeks later. The inauguration was to take place in village Assa Buttar in Faridkot district, a stronghold of the Chief Minister. The inauguration event included a large public meeting to be addressed by the Prime Minister and a pictorial display of the schemes of the programme. On the inauguration day, the Prime Minister arrived by helicopter looking very fit and erect, and much younger than his age.

After his public address, he was taken round the exhibition by the Chief Minister and me. The Chief Minister was trying to convey that he had been inspired by Schumacher's book *Small is Beautiful*, but there seemed to be no reaction from the Prime Minister. He was looking at a number of large photos of buffaloes that Punjab is famous for and he, known for his bluntness, turned around to the Chief Minister and exclaimed in Hindi, 'You drink buffalo milk!', and when the Chief Minister replied in the affirmative, the Prime Minister remarked, again in Hindi, 'That's why your brain thinks like a buffalo!' The Chief

Minister looked visibly embarrassed but just laughed it away. It was difficult for me to keep a straight face, standing between the two, so I quickly moved on to continue explaining the programme. This was my second meeting with Morarji Desai, the first being when as Deputy Prime Minister he visited the IAS Academy in Mussoorie. He was known to be outspoken and could often be very blunt, just like we witnessed in Asa Buttar.

When it came down to implementation of the programme, we encountered unexpected problems. The programme had been given wide publicity in the state and soon there was a clamour from villages for getting 'focal point' status. Political pressures started mounting on the Development Minister and he started declaring villages as 'focal points' almost as largesse and to spread his political patronage.

I protested to Bains, who after speaking to the minister, assured me that no such announcements would be made thereafter and we could proceed with implementation as per the plan. This assurance was belied when a few days later notes started coming again from the minister's office naming villages to be notified as 'focal points'. I sent these notes back to the minister with the remarks that '*as this was contrary to the understanding given to me by the minister, I'm returning the file for reconsideration*', and hence withheld notifying those villages as 'focal points'. The consequence of my resistance was that the minister started getting the villages notified as 'focal points' through the office of the Director, Panchayati Raj, who was a promotee IAS officer and on my questioning him, he readily admitted his subservience and thus helplessness in the matter.

Seeing no other alternative in that disgusting situation, I reverted to Bains and said that in view of the minister's intransigence and his own inability to effectively intervene in the matter, it had become untenable for me to continue. I had been happily working in the PSIDC but it was on his insistence that I had been given this assignment and could not be a passive witness to the distortion of the programme. I pleaded that if this was the way the programme was to be administered, there was no necessity to have involved me in its formulation and implementation. I, therefore, conveyed my intention to proceed on leave so that someone, who is probably more pliable, could be appointed in my place. This was perhaps the most disappointing turn of events during my career in the Punjab government.

But let me end this unfortunate episode on a more humorous note. The Integrated Rural Development Programme had been submitted to the National Planning Commission for Central government's financial assistance. For a long time there was no response, not even an acknowledgement from the Commission. When the matter was pursued, the relevant file was untraceable and after some searching it was found to have been missent to the Division dealing, inter alia with dairy development schemes. A senior officer in the concerned Division had cursorily reviewed the programme document and seeing the word 'Buttar' (the Prime Minister had inaugurated the programme in Assa Buttar), put a noting that since the proposal dealt with 'butter', it should be sent to the Division concerned with dairy development!

7

An Undramatic Interlude

Do not dwell in the past,
do not dream of the future,
concentrate the mind on the present moment.
—Buddha

I spent my leave mostly in Delhi, feeling a sense of disillusionment, and actually contemplated leaving the service. However, I returned to Chandigarh in 1978 after a period of about two months and was posted as Joint Secretary, Finance. It was my first posting in the Punjab secretariat and, as it turned out, my last. The job involved the usual work of a finance division, processing and approving expenditure proposals from other departments of the government. It was definitely a contrasting experience compared to my earlier assignments which were challenging, time-bound and action-oriented with more tangible outcomes. But much to my relief, this stint was free from the kind of tension that one had experienced earlier and it gave me the much needed exposure one must have to the functioning of the state secretariat. It also gave me the opportunity to get to know some of the luminaries of the Punjab cadre even though I had never worked with them. Among them were N.N. Vohra and Usha Vohra with their contrasting but equally effective styles of functioning. I looked at N.N. Vohra, whose career graph culminated as Governor of Jammu and Kashmir, as a role model who in meetings could inject humour into the most serious discussions with telling effect.

The year 1978 was also a time of considerable excitement in my personal life. We were expecting our first child. Shortly before the expected delivery date, Madhu had gone to Mumbai for the delivery as her mother wanted Dr Rusi Soonawala, famous gynaecologist and also a very close family friend, to handle the case. The due date was around my birthday, March 23, so I had planned to be in Mumbai a few days earlier. As it transpired, I was in Delhi en route to Mumbai, having a drink in the evening with my father-in-law on 19 March 1978 when we got the news that Madhu had to undergo an emergency caesarean and had given birth to a girl. I was relieved that they both were well and delighted that my Ravina was born.

I had wanted a daughter and had told Madhu that I would like to name her Ravina. When I arrived at the hospital the next day, my mother-in-law showed me a list of names she had selected for the baby but none of them appealed to me. The name Ravina was not in the list. Without getting into any argument, I added the name 'Ravina' at the bottom of the list. When Vyjayanthimala, the renowned film actress, who was also a close family friend, dropped in to see Madhu, my mother-in-law handed over the list of names to her to get her view. Much to my relief, she exclaimed, 'Ravina is such an unusual and lovely name'. That clinched the matter and about a week later we were back in Chandigarh with our daughter Ravina.

Chandigarh was the ideal city to live in and bring up a family, especially with our spacious dwelling. The city's pleasant environment and modern infrastructure made it even more attractive and liveable. Moreover, our large house was ideally suited to bringing up our newborn daughter. In a few months, Ravina loved being taken out into the large garden and watch the four poodles frolicking. They were very gentle with the baby and could be safely left sitting on the same bed without any fear. Ravina was a colic baby and her attacks would normally come in the evenings. I would jocularly remark that her colic hour would often clash with our cocktail hour! We accidentally discovered that taking her out for a drive would immediately work wonders to stop her crying, so a short evening drive became almost a daily routine. Ravina seemed to have an ear for music as early as when she was kicking her legs in a cycling motion in the cradle. She seemed to enjoy listening to the song, 'Brown Girl in the Ring'. She would react with a soft '*um*' sound whenever there was a pause in the song.

Notwithstanding all these comforts, we decided to shift to Delhi after about a year. I opted for deputation to the Central government. My name was circulated among the various ministries and S.S. Puri, who had recently moved to the post of Secretary, Planning Commission, selected me, being aware of my experience in the formulation of the Integrated Rural Development Programme when he was Chief Secretary, Punjab. Prior to our departure for Delhi, Sunny, in whose house we were living, offered to sell his house to us. He was facing financial problems and so it was a kind of distress sale at a price much below what might be the market price. It was a very tempting offer especially as it was prime property and we had enjoyed living there for so many years. But my conscience wouldn't permit me to take advantage of a good friend's difficult situation. I told him that as the market price of the house was much more, I would assist him in the sale of the house. As it transpired, we left for Delhi and soon thereafter Sunny sold the house and handed over possession to the buyer and with that went all my furniture that I had left behind.

I was appointed Deputy Secretary, Land Reforms, in the Planning Commission. After joining, I called on Puri who confirmed that he had selected me based on my experience in rural development in Punjab. I was happy to meet a batchmate S.K. Duggal, who by virtue of his ex-army seniority, was there as Director but in a different Division.

Immediately after Independence, the Central government decided to implement comprehensive agrarian reform measures. The land reform had four main components: abolition of intermediaries (zamindari system) and transferring land to actual cultivators; tenancy reforms to regulate rent, provide security of land tenure, and confer ownership rights to tenants; imposing ceilings on landholdings and redistribute the excessive land to the landless on a more equitable basis; and consolidation of landholdings to make farming more efficient and productive. As I settled into my work, I realized that the land reforms were, in a sense, a very light charge and at times appeared more of an academic exercise. Unlike my earlier assignments, there was limited scope for achieving tangible results.

The Central government, as a policy, had been advocating land reforms for decades but in many states it remained politically a highly sensitive issue. Moreover, the implementation of related legislation was a matter within the realm of the state governments and the Central government could at best play an advocacy role and monitor the progress of implementation in the states. The only states to have taken up land reforms with some seriousness were West Bengal and Kerala, both under CPI (M)-led governments. Punjab and Haryana had legislated to make consolidation of landholdings compulsory as majority of farmers in these states had small or fragmented landholdings. Most of the other states had merely indulged in political rhetoric. Meetings with state governments were convened periodically to review progress of implementation of land reforms and we would go through the motions of discussing the virtues of land reforms, knowing fully well that many states were just paying lip service to it. This became a highly frustrating time in the office and invariably, I would return home feeling very exhausted, certainly not from overwork but more from the futility of it. I had been in the Planning Commission for about a year when there was a major political change in the country.

Prime Minister Morarji Desai resigned in mid-July 1979. With the outside support of the Congress, Charan Singh, a popular farmer leader, was then sworn in as the Prime Minister on 28 July 1979. However, a day before the meeting of Parliament, the Congress withdrew its support, and after just 23 days in power, Charan Singh resigned. Indira Gandhi returned to power with a thumping majority in January 1980. Subsequently, the Akali–Janata Party government in Punjab was dismissed in early 1980 and the state was placed under President's rule. Giani Zail Singh, former Chief Minister of Punjab, was the Home Minister of India and, ably assisted by a shrewd Punjab cadre officer, S.P. Bagla was directly overseeing administrative changes in Punjab. He called me and said he wanted me to return to Punjab. He was the Chief Minister during my stint in the PSIDC and so, being familiar with my work there, he suggested that I go back to the PSIDC as Managing Director. I indicated my disinclination to return to the PSIDC and expressed my preference to go to a district as Deputy Commissioner, an assignment I had not done so far. He suggested Patiala, knowing my links with the Patiala family, which I declined, thinking of the potential conflict of interest that could arise. The Home Minister then left it to me to choose the district and I indicated Ludhiana, knowing its importance in the state. Within a short time my posting orders were issued and I returned to Punjab as Deputy Commissioner, Ludhiana.

This change coincided with the arrival of our second child. As the delivery date was just a couple of months away, I deferred my move to Ludhiana to March 1980 with the family to follow later. This time the delivery was in Delhi and the highly trusted doctor and family friend, Dr Rusi Soonawala, came from Mumbai along with anaesthetist Dr Honagiri as my mother-in-law had little faith in the doctors in Delhi! Madhu and I had again pre-selected the name, Aushima, in the expectation of another daughter. We had attended a wedding in Hoshiarpur of Dr Choudhary's daughter Oshima. We liked that name and decided that if we had another daughter, we would name her, albeit spelled differently, Aushima. As Madhu was to undergo caesarean again, the date was fixed in advance for the two doctors to be in Delhi and I, too, could be in Delhi on the day of delivery. On 4 April 1980, we were blessed with a beautiful baby girl with striking sharp features and so very appropriately we named her Aushima. Soon after that, Madhu joined me in Ludhiana with our two babies and of course along came the poodles.

8

Punjab in Turmoil: The Bhindranwale Factor

The most difficult thing is the decision to act,
the rest is merely tenacity.
The fears are paper tigers.
You can do anything you decide to do.
You can act to change and control your life;
and the procedure, the process is its own reward.

—Amelia Earhart

Prime Minister's Visit

My immediate responsibility as Deputy Commissioner was to conduct the Assembly elections which were due in June 1980. The Akali Dal, having had its government dismissed, was in a belligerent mood and the contest with the Congress was expected to be close as well as acrimonious. Prime Minister Indira Gandhi was to visit Ludhiana to address an election rally, so the local Congress leaders were feverishly working to ensure a sizable turnout. It was also an opportunity for them to demonstrate their loyalty to the party and project their credentials as a strong candidate for consideration at the time of government formation. The Prime Minster was to arrive by helicopter and arrangements were made for the helicopter to land on the grounds of Government College for Women. The election rally was to be held in the stadium, which could accommodate the expected large numbers and also was considered suitable from security aspects. There was a clamour among the Congress leaders to be present and be noted by the Prime Minister as soon as she arrived at the helipad.

We were, however, constrained in the interest of security to restrict the number of persons at the helipad, so we decided that only Darbara Singh, the leader of the Punjab Congress, would be there to receive the Prime Minister. The welcome party consisting of other aspiring leaders would receive her at the stadium. The reaction was, as expected, one of protest among these leaders as they were very keen to be seen as the Prime Minister stepped out of the helicopter. They met me as a delegation, some for the first time, insisting on a full-fledged welcome reception at the helipad. I emphasised that as far as security was concerned, there could be no compromise and that remained the district administration's primary consideration in making the arrangements. The Prime Minister's visit went off well and without any untoward incident. It was also an opportunity to establish my style of functioning as the district in charge and importantly, very early in my assuming charge. The ensuing elections were won by the Congress. Darbara Singh became Chief Minister and four of the eight cabinet ministers sworn in were from Ludhiana district.

Akali Dal Agitation; Bhindranwale's Detention

The installation of the Congress government in 1980 was followed by a politically tumultuous period in Punjab. The Akali Dal had launched a state-wide agitation under Sant Longowal for implementation of their demands listed in the Anandpur Sahib Resolution adopted by the Akalis in 1973. The Resolution, in essence, contained the following major demands:

a) Chandigarh originally raised as a capital for Punjab should be handed over to Punjab.
b) The long-standing demand of the Akali Dal for the merger in Punjab of the Punjabi-speaking areas, to be identified by linguistic experts with village as a unit, should be conceded.
c) The control of headworks should continue to be vested in Punjab and, if need be, the Reorganisation Act should be amended.
d) The arbitrary and unjust award given by Mrs Indira Gandhi during the Emergency on the distribution of Ravi-Beas waters should be revised on the universally accepted norms and principles, and justice be done to Punjab.
e) Keeping in view the special aptitude and martial qualities of the Sikhs, the present ratio of their strength in the army should be maintained.
f) The excesses being committed on the settlers in the Terai region of the Uttar Pradesh in the name of land reforms should be vacated by making suitable amendments in the ceiling law on the Central guidelines.

Jarnail Singh Bhindranwale, who had risen from a Sikh preacher to become the head of the Damdami Taksal and who had earlier been propped up by the Congress to counter the Akali Dal's influence in the state, used that platform to emerge as the leader of a militant group and symbolised the extremist and terrorist movement in the state. He treated the Congress as his adversary and so made common cause with the Akalis to advocate the Anandpur Sahib Resolution. He moved around Punjab with his militant followers with impunity and several incidents of violence and acts of terrorism in the state were allegedly committed by Jarnail Singh Bhindranwale's followers.

In 1982, Bhindranwale and the Akali Dal launched the Dharam Yudh Morcha demanding fulfilment of the Anandpur Sahib Resolution, which in effect was aimed to grant regional autonomy to Punjab state within India. It was buttressed with populist demands attracting widespread support of people in Punjab, particularly the youth, who were dissatisfied with the prevailing economic, social, and political conditions. Through this movement Bhindranwale emerged as a leader of Sikh militancy. His followers targeted the Nirankaris and their well-known supporters, prominent among them being Lala Jagat Narain, the founder editor of the Jullundur-based Hind Samachar group of papers, which had a very wide circulation in the state. Narain's vernacular newspapers were openly critical of the militancy and terrorism in the state, which was attributed to Bhindranwale. At the same time, Narain strongly supported the Nirankaris, making him a prime target for the militant group.

Narain was travelling home one evening from Chandigarh to Jullundur when his car was attacked by a group of militants and he was killed. The incident took place while he was still in Ludhiana district, very close to the Jullundur district boundary near Phillaur. As soon as I was informed of the incident, D.R. Bhatti, Senior Superintendent of Police (SSP), and I rushed to the site to find Narain's bullet-riddled body lying on the back seat of the car. We took the body to the hospital in Ludhiana and soon the news of his assassination spread throughout the city. By nightfall a large crowd, mainly supporters of the Bharatiya Janata Party (BJP) incensed over the murder of the widely respected journalist, had gathered at the hospital premises shouting slogans and threatening retaliation. A little later, we were informed that a *bandh* had been declared next day in Ludhiana city and plans were being made to carry Narain's body in a procession through the city. In the highly charged atmosphere, this would have definitely led to intensifying tension and inevitable violence in the city.

The SSP expressed his apprehension that a very large response to the call for observing a *bandh* was imminent and already announcements were being made throughout the city to shut down shops and exhorting people to join the procession. Taking stock of this volatile situation, we discussed various measures for diffusing the situation including a late night meeting with leaders but the feedback we got was that they were adamant about taking out Narain's body in a procession. His outspoken writings in the *Hind Samachar* against the extremist elements in the state had made him immensely popular as a symbol of a fightback to end their reign of terror, and they perceived this to be the cause for which he was martyred. Having considered various options, none of which seemed feasible, I said to Bhatti, 'Why don't we arrange to remove his body out of the district to his home in Jullundur immediately as that might diffuse the situation?' We eventually decided to proceed on my suggestion that we take pre-emptive action to transfer Narain's body to his home in Jullundur before daybreak. Without the body in Ludhiana, there would be no protest march and the impending catastrophe would be averted.

However, the body could not be moved from the hospital before a post-mortem was conducted. An inquest report was prepared as required under the Indian Criminal Procedure Code indicating the cause of unnatural death and I directed the doctors to conduct the post-mortem immediately. They initially expressed disinclination, citing relevant legal provisions, stating that a post-mortem could only be conducted in daylight. I asked them to produce the manual which, on perusal, I found contained a proviso allowing post-mortem to be conducted if the District Magistrate certified the adequacy of light to determine the cause of death. I explained to them that these instructions had been prepared years ago when lighting systems in hospitals were not so advanced which made it difficult to undertake forensic work to determine the real cause of death. However, the hospital was then adequately provided with modern lighting systems and I was ready to certify the adequacy of light for conducting the post-mortem. Moreover, as the inquest report had established that the cause of death was bullet wounds, the detection of colour changes in body tissues was not so critical. Based on my certification, post-mortem was conducted immediately in my presence and we were able to send the body to Jullundur well before daybreak. In the morning when the crowds turned up to take possession of the body, they were informed that it had already reached Narain's residence in Jullundur. The procession was called off and a potentially threatening and dangerously violent law and order situation was thereby avoided.

The murder of Lala Jagat Narain was alleged to have been carried out as per Bhindranwale's orders and the police was looking to arrest him on various allegations of violence. Bhindranwale offered to court arrest in Chowk Mehta, near Amritsar, if he was allowed to address a public gathering. It became a massive media event for the top leadership of the Akali Dal and thousands of Bhindranwale's followers gathered to hear his speech claiming innocence and to witness his surrender. Following his surrender, as apprehended, there was large-scale violence in different parts of Punjab. Hence, the government's decision to send him to Ludhiana for detention was a serious challenge to the district administration. He was transported from Chowk Mehta under strict security in a convoy of cars. It was considered imprudent to bring Bhindranwale into the city or to detain him in the district jail which was located in the heart of the city. We, therefore, planned with the government's approval, to surreptitiously separate his car from the convoy of police escort vehicles well before the convoy entered the city limits and divert it to an undisclosed government rest house in a secluded place. The welcome arches put up in the city and the large number of people gathered along the road to cheer him vindicated our plans.

However, just about 30 minutes before the expected arrival of the convoy at the spot from where we were to divert his car, SSP Bhatti came to me to convey a message from the Director General of Police that Bhindranwale's car should be allowed to go through the city. He could not explain why this obviously senseless change was made. I immediately telephoned Chief Minister Darbara Singh, who was in Chandigarh, and asked him why this carefully thought-out plan had suddenly been aborted. The Chief Minister sounded very agitated and all he said was that this was not his decision but the orders had come directly from Home Minister Zail Singh. Following these orders, Bhindranwale's convoy was taken through the city including Bhindranwale's car. As apprehended, there was a public procession following the convoy which became progressively larger as it went through the city with people in different modes of transport joining it and shouting pro-Bhindranwale slogans. When we reached the designated place of his detention, there was no secrecy left.

Escorting Bhindranwale from Chowk Mehta to Ludhiana was a senior IPS officer, Chahal, Senior Superintendent of Police, Gurdaspur district. He had come with a set of instructions regarding the treatment to be meted out to Bhindranwale while in detention. Bhindranwale was still sitting in the Ambassador car with two companions when Chahal came across to where the Deputy Inspector General, Police, Patiala Range, SSP Bhatti and I were discussing security arrangements to convey the instructions which, he said, were agreed conditions attached to his surrender.

1. Two companions—his cook and his *sewak*—would stay with him
2. When he is interrogated, it must be only by a *gursikh* (a Sikh who observes all five tenets of Sikhism)
3. When he is interrogated, he should be sitting at the same level or higher but not lower than the interrogator and
4. If he chooses not to answer any question, no third degree method should be used.

I listened aghast and quipped to Chahal, 'Who is under arrest, Bhindranwale or the Punjab government?' I then turned to Bhatti and said that as far as I was concerned, Bhindranwale was someone under arrest and should accordingly be treated as one under detention. I did not think it necessary to personally confront Bhindranwale that evening at the place of detention or even thereafter. I deputed Ludhiana Sub Divisional Magistrate, Hardial Singh, a seasoned Provincial Civil Service officer who was on his final posting before retirement, to visit the rest house daily and give me a report on the security situation there. The rest house had virtually become a place of pilgrimage with scores of people visiting it every day to see the place where Bhindranwale had been detained. In fact, the road leading to the rest house was soon lined with food and refreshment vendors serving the visiting public.

After about a week or so, it came to my attention that each time Hardial Singh went to meet Bhindranwale, as part of his daily visit, he would pay his respects by touching Bhindranwale's knees. So the next time Hardial Singh came to me with his report, I asked him to give me a minute-to-minute account of his visit and when he omitted to say anything on his mode of greeting, I confronted him with a direct question on how he greeted Bhindranwale. He was still evasive, so I asked him a more direct question whether he greeted him by touching his knees, a traditional mode of greeting to express respect. With folded hands, Hardial Singh admitted that out of respect for 'Santji', he did bow before him and touched his knees. I admonished him reminding him that as he was representing me, his action was tantamount to my touching Bhindranwale's knees, and as I represented the government, that in turn meant the government was paying respects to a person under detention on a murder charge.

The situation had become untenable and relocating Bhindranwale became imperative. I telephoned the Sub Divisional Magistrate of Samrala, Rakesh Singh, a young IAS officer who was on his first posting, and told him that I was transferring Bhindranwale to his charge with confidence that he would treat him as was his due as a detainee. Bhindranwale was accordingly shifted and detained in a rest house in Samrala subdivision but, as secrecy around his place of detention had already been compromised, the crowds followed him there too. I then wrote to the government that it was becoming increasingly difficult in terms of security to keep Bhindranwale in detention in the rest house and recommended he be sent to a regular jail. The jail in Ludhiana, located in the heart of the city, was not suitable for this purpose. Bhindranwale was eventually shifted to the jail in Ferozepur from where he was subsequently set free for want of evidence to prove the murder charge against him. Acquitted of the murder charge,

Bhindranwale secured himself in the Golden Temple in Amritsar.

The political atmosphere in Punjab remained tense with the Akalis intensifying their agitation against the Congress and communal clashes taking place across the state. Apprehending further escalation of communal tension, Section 144 CrPC was imposed in Ludhiana to prevent violence. This prohibitory order prevented the gathering of five or more persons and empowered the law enforcing authority to take whatever preventive action it deemed necessary for the maintenance of law and order. Peace in Ludhiana, being an important and flourishing commercial city, was of critical importance as any untoward incident there could cascade into violence across the state. I was on a round of the city checking the law and order situation when SSP Bhatti informed me that four Congress ministers, hailing from Ludhiana, were planning to take out an all-party peace march through Chowra Bazar, which is the commercial hub of the city. They, along with local leaders of other political parties including Akali MLAs, had already assembled at the Ghanta Ghar Chowk, which was to be the starting point of their ill-conceived peace march. I immediately went to them and told them that as prohibitory orders were in force, we could not permit them to take out the peace march, however well-intended it might be. To me it appeared to be an attempt at seeking self-importance and just a photo opportunity to get publicity.

My refusal to allow the peace march incensed the ministers and in particular, Joginder Pal Pandey, who had taken this initiative and was the most enthusiastic to lead the peace march. He telephoned the Chief Minister and complained that I was not cooperating in their holding the peace march. He then passed the phone to me expecting the Chief Minister to direct me to cooperate with them. I explained to the Chief Minister that taking out a peace march was unnecessary as everything was under control, and on the other hand, it was fraught with danger of creating alarm and escalating tension among the public with the added risk of miscreants creating mischief when the procession passed through sensitive areas. The Chief Minister agreed with my assessment and left it to me to decide. I accordingly reiterated my stand against any procession. The peace march had to be aborted, much to the chagrin of the ministers. They were, however, determined and decided to shift the peace march to another city, and Patiala became the venue. As apprehended, there was violence and about 200 shops were burnt during the so-called peace march in Patiala. This incident underscored the imperative that when prohibitory orders under Section 144 CrPC are imposed, the district administration must strictly enforce them and make no exceptions even under political pressure, as it is ultimately the responsibility of the administration should there be any mishap.

A salutary effect of this incident was that the leaders of other political parties, particularly the Akalis, who had gathered there for the all-party peace march, having witnessed the district administration withstanding political pressure being exerted by ministers, developed full confidence in the impartiality of the district administration and thereafter were very forthcoming in extending their cooperation to the district administration whenever it was warranted.

The Akalis were trying to give a greater impetus to their agitation and they were encouraged by the support they were getting from the more militant groups, particularly from Bhindranwale under the banner of their Dharam Yudh Morcha. Their agitation had started targeting public services. A 'rasta roko' call was made to stop movement of traffic on the Grand Trunk (G.T.) Road, which is the main arterial road of the state. The government had issued instructions to district administrations to ensure no such blockage of traffic took place. I met with Akali leaders in advance and told them that while the government instructions were to prevent and remove any gathering causing blockage of roads, I would not forcibly disband a gathering as long as they assured me that it remained peaceful and vehicles should be allowed uninterrupted passage. It must be assumed that the people travelling were for some emergency purpose, as they would normally desist from travelling by road on that day.

On the 'rasta roko' day, a large congregation, mostly of women and children, had squatted on the G.T. Road to Jullundur. I went across to them to get reassurance of my understanding with their leaders, which they confirmed. There was virtually no traffic but the very few vehicles that did brave the threat were given uninterrupted passage. The Director General of Police, who was surveying the situation in the state by helicopter, observed large gathering near Ludhiana city and ordered the SSP to immediately take forcible action to clear the squatters. The SSP came to me with the DGP's orders to take forcible action. I told him to inform the DGP that as he would have noted, there was no vehicle stopped, and so there was no need to take such precipitous action. While clashes were reported from other districts, there was no untoward incident in Ludhiana district. Often, a purpose can be achieved more effectively by means other than just the use of force, as we were able to demonstrate in this case.

Next came the Akalis' call for 'rail roko', announcing a day when they would ensure no trains ran in the state. The Union Home Ministry took serious cognisance of this call as it was targeting a national public service. A meeting was held in the Home Ministry which was attended by the Chief Minister and senior officials from the Punjab government. As a follow-up and as an indication of the seriousness, the Union government was attaching to ensuring there was no disruption of rail services, the Home Ministry deputed Nayyar, Special Secretary Home Ministry, to hold a meeting with the Punjab government in Chandigarh to which all District Magistrates and Police Chiefs were summoned. He came with a clear message that the Union government would not submit to the 'rail roko' call so 'trains must run', regardless of what the Akalis might try to do to disrupt services.

I was bemused by this curt message with no suggestion on how we could frustrate the attempts of the agitators to disrupt train services. I, therefore, stood up and presented a scenario for Nayyar to advise how we should deal with it. As we had witnessed during the 'rasta roko' episode, it would be largely women and children from villages adjoining the railway track squatting on the railway track, ostensibly holding prayer gatherings. This could not be prevented as we did not have adequate police force to safeguard the entire length of the railway track. Any attempt by the skeleton police force to remove the squatters would be resisted and if force was used, the crowd would retaliate by attacking the police force with stone ballast, lying all along the track. Hence, my question to Nayyar was, what specific action would he suggest in that situation. If 'trains must run' at any cost, would he suggest trains running over the squatters, something that would be reminiscent of the dastardly actions under the colonial regime. There was no response and I could see Chief Minister Darbara Singh nodding his head in approval of my intervention. Nayyar finally mumbled something inaudible and then reiterated the Union government's determination to not let the Akalis succeed in stopping train services.

I then ventured to make a suggestion which I thought would be a face-saving for the government in thwarting the 'rail roko' call. I pointed out that Punjab is connected by rail only through the Ambala-Rajpura link. The night before the 'rail roko' a goods train should be derailed on this link, making it look like an act of sabotage. This derailment would ostensibly become the reason for trains not running pre-empting claims of success of the 'rail roko' call and at the same time, it would be a face-saving for the government. In that situation, public perception would be sympathetic to the government and against the Akalis, for the derailed train could have been a passenger train resulting in loss of life. There was no direct response to my suggestion at the meeting but during the tea after the meeting, the Chief Minister said to me that he was glad I had raised the issue as, in the previous meeting in Delhi, they could not say anything. My proposed strategy was, however, not resorted to. I can only surmise that my suggestion required effort that was beyond what they were willing to put in to ward off the 'rail roko' call and the day did pass without trains running in Punjab.

There were other occasions too, when I as District Magistrate did not agree with the state headquarters assessment of the situation and so did not follow their directives. As the Akali agitation appeared to be gathering greater momentum, the state government decided to have the army do flag marches in every district headquarters. Lt Gen. Rodney Hira, GOC XI Corps, posted in Jullundur, who I had met during my army attachment, came to Ludhiana to discuss the details for the flag march. While I was certainly delighted to meet him again, I told him that the situation in my district was normal and the civil administration was in full control of the situation. I was, therefore, not in favour of an army flag march, as it might surcharge the atmosphere with tension and heighten a false sense of fear and insecurity. We spent the evening enjoying a drink together and reminiscing about our first meeting in Rangia.

However, the next day I received a telephone call from A.K. Sen, Commissioner, Jullundur Division, questioning my decision against the flag march. I was taken aback as Ludhiana district is administratively not part of Jullundur Division and, therefore, not under his charge. I normally showed due deference to my senior colleagues but if someone tried to give me unsolicited directions on how to do my job, especially without locus standi, I had no hesitation in pointing this out. I, therefore, responded firmly to the Commissioner asserting that as District Magistrate of Ludhiana, it was my responsibility to decide and not take directions from extraneous sources especially when it was not backed by accountability. We ended the short conversation with the Commissioner warning me that by not following the government's directive, my post could be in jeopardy. Fortunately, Ludhiana district remained peaceful and I stood vindicated.

On another occasion, the state government, having decided to take a more hard-line approach in dealing with the Akali agitation, directed all districts to impose prohibitory orders under Section 144 Cr PC on the occasion of Guru Nanak's birthday, which is traditionally celebrated with great fervour through religious processions and *langars* (free kitchens). Being cognisant that imposition of prohibitory orders would not prevent the taking out of processions and hence enforcement would be extremely difficult, I decided against the imposition of prohibitory orders. Instead, I met with senior Sikh leaders in Ludhiana, and confided to them that I would not follow the government's directive to impose prohibitory orders and instead would facilitate their taking out of a procession, even joining the procession myself, provided I had their firm assurance that it would remain a strictly religious procession without any political undertones and violence. Some of the leaders present were previously witness to the firm and impartial stand I had taken at the time of the planned peace march, and having resisted pressure exerted by the Congress ministers. They expressed confidence in me and readily gave me their assurance. I did not impose prohibitory orders while in all other districts the DMs issued prohibitory orders. The Commissioner, Patiala Division, called me to enquire why I had not done so, and I reiterated my position and assured him that as it was my responsibility, I was ready to be held accountable for my decision.

On Guru Nanak's birthday, the religious procession was taken out, starting from the main Gurdwara Kalgidar. Apparently some younger participants out of youthful exuberance took out *kirpans* from the Gurdwara and started shouting political slogans. The senior leaders, true to their assurance to me, dissuaded them with the threat that they would themselves withdraw from the procession if their commitment to me was not honoured. On my part, as I had assured them, I joined the procession and it went through the city peacefully as a religious procession and without any untoward incident. In all other districts, where prohibitory orders were imposed, attempts by administration to stop processions only resulted in avoidable clashes and a strong public reaction against the perceived insensitivity of the administration to the religious sentiments of the Sikhs.

The next stage of intensifying the agitation was 'jail bharo', calling on all Akali supporters to court arrest as a sign of protest over their demands not being met by the Congress government. The entire senior Akali leadership decided to court arrest in Ludhiana. As the central jail was not suitable because of its location as well as in accommodating the expected large numbers, we converted part of a government housing complex under construction into a temporary jail. The area was cordoned off by barbed wire and arrangements for water and sanitation were made on an emergency basis. On the appointed day, we herded the hordes to the temporary jail.

A few days later, I visited Parkash Singh Badal, former Chief Minister, in the jail. It was more of a courtesy call, considering Badal's status as a former Chief Minister who was now a political prisoner. A number of other prominent Akali leaders including MLAs were also there. Badal had a large room to himself and appeared to be well provided for with baskets of fruits, vegetables and regular tea service. He offered me a cup of tea and it was the first of several visits I made, talking to Badal over a cup of tea.

On one such visit, Badal took me into confidence and said he wanted to meet and negotiate with the Congress in order to end the impasse, but it had to be directly with a member of the Gandhi family. He said that the Congress should not think that they had vanquished the Akalis just because they were all in jail. They should understand that if the more moderate leadership that he represented lost its credibility, and referring to Bhindranwale, he said 'that coward sitting in the Golden Temple' would gain ascendancy. He wanted it to be a one-on-one meeting and did not want any other Akali leader to know, as he was aware that many among them were hardliners and would never agree to his initiative for talks. I assured him that I would communicate his message to the right quarters.

I used my college days' association with Rajiv Gandhi and my close friendship with Arun Singh to convey Badal's message. Rajiv was then General Secretary of the Congress and Arun had been appointed Parliamentary Secretary. More importantly, they both were very close friends. I telephoned Arun and he agreed to convey Badal's message to Rajiv. A few days later, Arun reverted to me with a positive response, namely the Prime Minister had approved Rajiv meeting Badal. As we planned, Rajiv would travel incognito to Ludhiana. I conveyed this to Badal and discussed with him my planned arrangements for the meeting. Since both sides desired complete secrecy, I had planned a two-hour blackout late at night in Ludhiana city, during which time Badal would be taken out of the jail and brought to my residence to meet Rajiv. Thereafter, he would return to jail before his absence was noticed. All the arrangements were firmed up including a continental cuisine dinner for Rajiv, prepared a day in advance by Madhu, as she was going to be in Delhi on the appointed day.

When everything seemed to be on track as planned, came the anti-climax just the night before. Arun called me to say that Rajiv could not come because he had been asked by the Prime Minister to attend the Farnborough air show in the United Kingdom. In his place, Swaran Singh was being deputed to meet Badal. In great disappointment, I reiterated that Badal had emphatically stated that he was not going to meet anyone but a member of the Gandhi family, so Swaran Singh should not be sent. I also told Arun that I was not going to give this story to Badal as it was patently unconvincing. On my insisting that he give me the real reason so I could then decide how to deal with the matter with Badal, Arun said that close advisors of the Prime Minister had cautioned her against negotiating with Badal especially at this stage as they felt the Akalis were down and out. I conjectured that these close advisors must have been P.C. Alexander, Principal Secretary to the Prime Minister, and Krishnaswamy Rao Sahib, Cabinet Secretary, both of whom, I was convinced, had no clue of the Sikh psyche. History has shown that the Sikh is ready to fight for his rights till the end and can only be won over through appeasement. Tragically, a great opportunity to end the conflict was senselessly aborted which perhaps could have avoided the more tragic events that were to follow.

I got involved in yet another attempt to bring about a rapprochement between the Congress and the Akalis about a year later when, on my request, I was transferred to Delhi on deputation to the Central government. Madhu's brother Kavi passed away prematurely at the young age of 29 years leaving the family completely distraught, so we thought we should be with them in Delhi. We moved to Delhi mid-1983 and soon thereafter, I got involved in a series of backchannel discussions conducted by my father-in-law Romesh Bhandari, who was then Secretary, Economic Relations in MEA. On behalf of the Akali team, the interlocutor was Balwant Singh, former Finance Minister of Punjab. The meetings were held in secret at Mr Bhandari's residence, normally late in the evenings. The whole process was kept so discreet that media had no clue. After several meetings we were able to work out the broad contours of a rapprochement between the Congress and the Akalis.

Mr Bhandari informed the Prime Minister who then deputed the then Finance Minister Pranab Mukherjee to review the draft memorandum. Mukherjee came to Mr Bhandari's residence late one night and we discussed the draft agreement with him. His reaction was positive and he said he would 'show it to Madam'. We waited in great hope for a breakthrough but only to be disappointed again. It seemed that the same coterie of advisors had once again prevailed upon the Prime Minister against any action that might lead to resurgence of the Akalis in Punjab.

I have often wondered what course history might have taken had the Prime Minister responded positively to these initiatives. A rapprochement between the Congress and the Akalis would certainly have marginalised and diminished the influence Bhindranwale and his militants were exerting, thereby putting an end to extremism in the state and possibly, Operation Blue Star and the consequential tragic events in its aftermath might never have happened.

Some Extraordinary Anecdotes

As Deputy Commissioner, I was fortunate to enjoy the full confidence of Chief Minister Darbara Singh. This not only made it easier for me to resist political pressures sought to be exerted by any of the four ministers belonging to Ludhiana district, but also to function in an independent, impartial and apolitical manner. Whenever Darbara Singh visited Ludhiana, which was quite often and at times with no particular official commitment, all four ministers would invariably be present at the PWD Rest House to receive him. They perceived it to be an opportunity to get the Chief Minister's attention to issues they might not have been able to do in Chandigarh. But Darbara Singh would invariably give short shrift to their attempts to get his ear. Within a few minutes of his arrival, he would signal to me to leave with him. Often it was to one of the other rest houses or the government's tourist resort just outside the city. Over a cup of tea and, at times, *jalebies*, we would discuss a wide range of matters.

In one such meeting, I brought to his attention that a particular minister was contriving to grab land belonging to a *gaushala*, which was located in the heart of the city and so extremely valuable. I wanted him to know in advance that I was going to thwart that attempt. His response, as I had expected, was to give me the go-ahead. On a subsequent visit, Darbara Singh asked me about this case and I confirmed that I had thwarted the attempted takeover. He remarked with a wry smile that at a recent cabinet meeting he had remarked that it had come to his notice that a minister was trying to grab *gaushala* land in Ludhiana, glancing at the particular minister, and who, therefore, looked visibly embarrassed. On another occasion, just a few days after highly reputed DIG Avtar Singh Atwal was brutally murdered by Bhindranwale's militants on the threshold of the Golden

Temple, I remarked that it would have been the ideal opportunity to take punitive action against Bhindranwale, who was then ensconced in the Golden Temple, as such action would have received widespread public support and sympathy since a devout Sikh had been killed when he went to the holiest of Sikh shrines to pray. Darbara Singh nodded in agreement but said it was a matter on which decision could have been taken only by Union Home Minister Giani Zail Singh. Quite clearly, that was yet another example where the tenuous relationship between the two impacted on Darbara Singh's authority and his ability to handle effectively difficult political situations in the state.

In the midst of this politically charged atmosphere, the Congress Working Committee decided to hold a major political rally in Delhi in support of Prime Minister Indira Gandhi. The four ministers from Ludhiana were actively involved in mobilising people and material for the rally. One day I received a message to come to the PWD Rest House where I found the four ministers sitting with the three Assistant Excise and Taxation Commissioners posted in Ludhiana. I could immediately anticipate the purpose of my being called to that meeting. The ministers had asked the three officers to assist in mobilising monetary support for the rally and in response, they had expressed their inability till the matter was first cleared with me.

I had given standing instructions to all officers in the district that if they were ever asked to do something that was beyond their official duties, they were to decline and ask that the matter be first cleared with me as the Deputy Commissioner. I had assured the officers that I would protect them to the hilt from any fallout of their refusal, but if I found anyone breaching that code of conduct, I would not spare him. The ministers, therefore, called me to explain that they had to make various arrangements for the ensuing rally, including transport and

The author (second from left) with his parents and younger brothers in 1959

The author (right) with his parents, brothers and his wife 43 years later in 2002

(Clockwise from top left): The author (centre) at the victory ceremonies after the athletics finals at Bishop Cotton School, Shimla, in 1955, 1957, 1958 and 1959

The author (centre) as defendant in Gilbert & Sullivan's opera 'Trial by Jury' at Bishop Cotton School, Shimla, in 1959

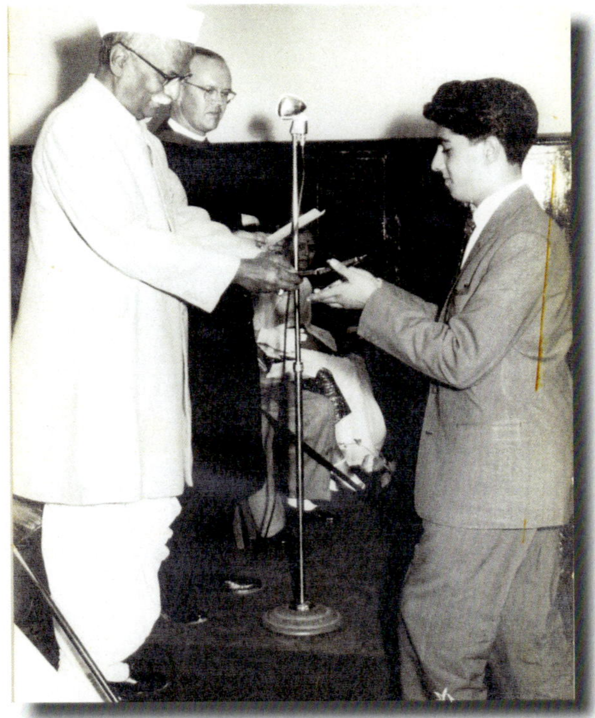

Receiving the President's Medal from President of India Dr Rajendra Prasad at Bishop Cotton School, Shimla, in July 1960

The author (sitting on the floor) during a rare revelry at LBSNAA, Mussoorie, in December 1968

The author (second from right) after receiving the Director's Medal for Physical Fitness from Deputy Prime Minister Morarji Desai at LBSNAA in 1969

Visiting a housing complex project in Kuwait undertaken by a PSIDC-promoted company, Punjab Chemiplants Ltd, in 1975

Escorting Prime Minister Indira Gandhi and Punjab Chief Minister Giani Zail Singh to the Punjab Pavilion at the Congress Session in Chandigarh in December 1976

(ABOVE): The author with his parents during the *sehra bandhi* ceremony before his marriage to Madhu in Delhi on 7 February 1977
(LEFT): With his bride Madhu during the wedding rituals

(Above): The author and his wife at a reception hosted for Prince Charles during his visit to Ludhiana in 1981.
(Right): The author with Prince Charles

Mother Teresa with the author's wife Madhu (above) and daughter Ravina when she visited his home in Ludhiana in 1982

Inmates from the Senior Citizens Home, Ludhiana attending the author's birthday party on 23 March 1982

Children evacuated from the leper colony and provided boarding and schooling at Bal Bhawan by the District Red Cross Society in Ludhiana in 1982

As member of the Indian delegation to the UNESCAP Commission Session, greeting Thailand Prime Minister Prem Tinsulanonda in Bangkok in 1984

Signing and exchange of the first trade protocol between India and China on 15 August 1984. The author is on the extreme left

Representing India at the annual ESCAP Commission Session in Bangkok in 1985

Jointly inaugurating the Indian Light Engineering Goods Exhibition, along with the Indian Ambassador to Japan and JETRO president, in Tokyo in 1986

With Chinese Premier Li Peng (second from right) at the Great Hall of the People, Beijing in October 1989

The author and his wife at the Asian Silk Fair, organised by UNESCAP, in Messe Berlin, Germany in October 1990

UN Secretary-General Boutros Boutros-Ghali (second from left) with the author during his visit to UNESCAP in 1992

Representing UNESCAP at UNCTAD VIII held in Cartagena de Indias, Columbia in February 1992

Being received by the host at the meeting of the Steering Group for Regional Economic Cooperation in Tehran in 1994

As Director, International Trade and Investment Division, UNESCAP, addressing a business conference organised by the Confederation of Asia-Pacific Chambers of Commerce and Industry in Taipei, Taiwan

ABOVE: Greeting Fidel V. Ramos, President of the Philippines, on the occasion of ASPAT'96 in Manila on 5 November 1996. LEFT: At a dinner with Mr Ramos the same day

The author (extreme right) at the World Council of Religious Leaders Board meeting in Singapore in July 2007

With Ban Ki-moon, Secretary-General of the United Nations, during his visit to Bangkok in 2008

Over the years, the author as administrator and diplomat

The author with his brothers and spouses during the wedding celebration of his daughter Aushima in Thailand in February 2013

The author, his wife Madhu and his mother-in-law Kumudesh Bhandari (extreme left) at a dinner hosted by Her Majesty Queen Sirikit of Thailand in February 2014

Her Majesty Queen Sirikit of Thailand explaining the relics collected by her for display in the Grand Palace

Receiving a gift, 'Power of Love' from Her Majesty Queen Sirikit of Thailand

Happy reunion with Amitabh Bachchan and Jaya at IIFA 2018 in Bangkok

The author reminiscing with Milkha Singh on their past association, in Delhi in December 2018

A Sunday outing with grandchildren Riana and Aryan

The author and his wife at their Bangkok home

A family get-together during the author's wife Madhu's birthday in Bangkok on 8 December 2021

rations and so needed assistance of the officers to mobilise finances.

I told the ministers in a polite but firm tone that I was not going to allow this, especially as I was aware that rations had already been collected from traders and even voluntary financial contributions had been made for the rally. Hence, I insisted there was no need to involve government officers in that effort. I, therefore, emphatically stated that I would not permit any officers getting involved in the collection of money as it would not only bring the district administration into disrepute but officers involved could be exposing themselves to accusations of having personally benefited in the process.

I added that I was aware that the District Transport Office had already given assistance in mobilising trucks through the local transport union, but the cost of diesel would have to be borne by the Congress so leaving them to ensure that the trucks were properly utilised. The ministers were livid as they were perhaps facing a situation they were not accustomed to. It was Joginder Pal Pandey again who called the Chief Minister in my presence to complain that I was not extending cooperation for the rally. Handing over the phone to me, I reiterated my stand to the Chief Minister within the hearing distance of the ministers. The Chief Minister chose not to intervene in the matter, leaving it to me to deal with it as I deemed right. Through all these episodes, Ludhiana district remained relatively peaceful and free from any serious untoward incident, barring of course the initial assassination of Lala Jagat Narain, which happened to take place within the district boundaries. I believe that was because we were able to assess each situation correctly and did not think of resorting to force as the first and only means to deal with it. What was also of vital importance was the confidence the people and, more importantly, the Opposition parties had in the district administration and their willingness to extend cooperation whenever required. It was not because I had been born under lucky astrological signs, as people started attributing, that while there were clashes and violent incidents in other districts, Ludhiana comparatively remained peaceful and incident-free.

In the course of my court work, I came across a case that startled me immensely. It related to allotment of 'inferior evacuee land'. Under the government's policy, 'inferior evacuee land', that is land that had been evacuated during the Partition, was to be allotted to landless agricultural workers and all such allotment cases were to be confirmed by the Deputy Commissioner, exercising the powers of District Collector. The instant case before me was to confirm the allotment of large tracts of inferior evacuee land to one Joginder Singh and his son. On scrutiny, I found that the allottee was no other but the Financial Commissioner, Revenue, of Punjab. He was occupying one of the three senior most positions in the Punjab government. Belonging to a scheduled caste by itself did not qualify him to be an allottee, as by no stretch of imagination could he and his son be categorised as landless agricultural labourers.

I was so astonished at this blatant misuse of power by one of the senior most bureaucrats in the state that I quipped in my order cancelling the allotment that if the Financial Commissioner of Punjab were to be treated as a landless agricultural labourer, then that makes me wonder what would be my own status as an officer much junior to him! I had no trepidation in cancelling the allotment and that too with scathing remarks. I was ready to face any fallout but there was no reprisal from his side, perhaps because better sense prevailed that it would have exposed him even more. He, however, had the audacity to file an appeal against my order before Commissioner, Patiala Division, which was duly dismissed on merits. The Commissioner then happened to be a batchmate, so years later we jocularly discussed this matter.

An interesting aspect of being a Deputy Commissioner, especially in an important district, is that one gets to meet some very interesting celebrities. Ludhiana, as an important industrial centre and the location therein of the internationally renowned Punjab Agriculture University (PAU), had the occasional VVIP visitors. During my posting there, the most memorable visit was that of Prince Charles, the heir to the British throne, who came in 1981 for a day to visit PAU. He arrived at the Adampur Air Force base and as he alighted from the aircraft in his khaki outfit, walked up to the reception line and we shook hands, it immediately struck me that he was much shorter than I had imagined. During his tour of the PAU, he evinced keen interest in the research work being done by the university in plants and animal husbandry as well as the development and use of solar energy. There was the expected huge excitement and clamour for invitations to the evening reception we were hosting in Prince Charles' honour. Amidst all the strict protocol, it was refreshing to see a very informal and relaxed Prince Charles as he met with all those present at the reception. By the end of the visit, we had established a rapport where our conversation became almost as one between old friends and Madhu had a glorious time exchanging jokes with him.

Another royal visitor was the Queen Mother of Nepal who made a transit halt at the PAU. As per protocol, I called on her. The Nepalese senior Foreign Service officer accompanying her, Prabal Rana, happened to be from my alma mater, BCS, so it turned out to be a very pleasant meeting. The Queen Mother presented me a replica of the famous Pashupatinath Temple located in Kathmandu. I duly informed the government that I had received the gift and sought advice on what to do with it as under the rules, any gift received by an officer in the discharge of his duty, must be reported to the government and if the value of the gift was in excess of the prescribed limit, it had to be handed over to the government. The government's response, asking me the market price, left me perplexed as it was not something available in the market, nor could its value be assessed as it was enclosed in a sealed glass case. After protracted correspondence, the government appeared to have no option but to allow me to keep the gift.

Then there was the memorable visit of Mother Teresa. Her foundation Missionaries of Charity was keen to open a branch in Ludhiana and had requested the government to allocate a plot of land for this purpose. When the matter came to the attention of the Minister, local government, Sardari Lal Kapur, who hailed from Ludhiana, he expressed his disinclination to approve that proposal, being under the misconception that the organisation was just a cover-up for carrying out religious conversions. Later he discussed the matter with me and I prevailed upon him to permit me to extend the requested assistance. A team from the Missionaries of Charity arrived in Ludhiana and I showed them the plot which they gratefully approved. Mother Teresa came personally to Ludhiana and to my residence to express her gratitude. We felt most privileged and blessed to have her in our home and to have her showering her affection and blessings on our two babies, Ravina and Aushima.

Ludhiana is also the district where the headquarters of the Namdhari sect is located in Bhaini Sahib. One day I received a message from the Chief Minister asking me to meet him at Bhaini Sahib to discuss something urgent. When I arrived there, the Chief Minister was sitting with Satguru Jagjit Singhji, the religious head of the Namdharis. Satguruji had earlier indicated to the Chief Minister that the Namdharis were keen to have their representative H.S. Hanspal, who had been selected as candidate of the Congress, elected to the Rajya Sabha. However, there was an unexpected hitch as Hanspal was not on the Ludhiana voters list and as elections were due shortly, some way had to be found immediately to overcome this deficiency. I said this could be treated as an inadvertent act of omission and assured them that the needful would be done.

Prior to the elections, Hanspal's name was on the voters list and he was duly elected to the Rajya Sabha. Thereupon, a strong bond developed between Satguruji and me which continued till long after I left Ludhiana and even years later when I happened to move to Bangkok. There is a very strong and affluent Namdhari community in Bangkok and Satguru Jagjit Singhji visits them quite often. Each time he would invite me to his *satsang*, which was always attended by thousands of his followers, he would make me sit right next to him, much to the curiosity of all the Namdharis attending the *satsang*.

Red Cross Initiatives

Among more cherished memories of our time in Ludhiana was the work we did in the district Red Cross Society. The Society was almost dormant when we arrived there and by the time we left after about three and a half years, it had become a dynamic organisation and reputed for the pioneering work done and the institutions established. Madhu, as the chairperson of the Society, was the prime mover and took on the work of the Society with a missionary zeal. In this she was ably supported by a very dedicated Pritam Singh Chatwal, vice-president of the Society. My role, as president of the Society, was essentially to support the effort being put in by them and to give guidance when needed. The first task was to revive the Society in terms of its membership and finance. The membership drive was personally spearheaded by Madhu and proved very successful and linked to that, the financial situation also improved through voluntary donations. In order to ensure greater stability and regular inflow of funds, the Red Cross Bhawan was virtually rebuilt and shops were rented out taking full advantage of its prime location. The resultant stable financial position of the Society enabled us to strengthen the traditional activities, such as blood donation camps, family welfare camps, etc. The Society's work was duly acknowledged and we won several awards at the national level, including annual awards given by the President and Vice-President of India.

Having put the Society on a firm footing and built up a reputation as a dynamic organisation, we felt confident to devote attention to institution building to meet vital social needs of society. The first was the establishment of a Senior Citizens Home in Ludhiana. The initiative was novel especially for India where joint family system was still largely prevalent and the thought of putting old people in homes was perceived to be a very alien concept. The major difference in our concept was that it was a home where the elderly themselves would volunteer to live and spend the sunset of their lives in dignity, free from any guilt of being a burden on their children. It was not intended to be a home for the economic destitute and so conceptually, it would provide all the basic comforts one would expect in a home, with a modest financial contribution by the occupants. The cost per head, then estimated at Rs 600 per month, was shared equally by the Society and the occupant. Moreover and very importantly, the occupants would be involved in managing the home. We had overwhelming response to our advertisement not only from Punjab but also other states, including as far as Maharashtra.

In the first stage, we could accommodate only 11 persons, each in an independent room. Later, it was expanded to double its capacity. There was a gurdwara and a temple in the Home. In due course, we purchased a minibus to take the senior citizens for an outing. When not used, the minibus was made available to provide public transport to the airport so that a part of its maintenance costs could be met. Madhu would spend a good part of the day in the Home, overseeing its running and spending time with the occupants. On each senior citizen's birthday, we would have a birthday party attended by all the occupants. On my birthday they were all invited to a tea party at our residence. The occupants were so happy that some of them made significant financial donation during their lifetime or in their will. The reputation of the Home spread quickly and we had some foreign delegations visiting it to understand the concept and how it differed from the western model.

Setting up the Senior Citizens Home was a very satisfying experience but we also experienced the ugly side of human character. When one of the lady occupants passed away, we informed her family and relatives in Mumbai and Delhi. There was no response from Mumbai and the relatives in Delhi seemed too preoccupied to make the effort to come to Ludhiana to take charge of the body. They expressed their inability and wanted the Society to make arrangements to send the body to Delhi. Since we were her adopted family, we decided to conduct all the rituals in Ludhiana itself. Soon thereafter, correspondence started from both sections of her family in Delhi and Mumbai, laying claim to her possessions. The lady had bequeathed her savings to the Home, and quite understandably so. Many years later when Madhu and I visited the Home, there was just one occupant there from our time. He was a former freedom fighter and perhaps at that time the most stubborn and difficult person we had to deal with. He was bedridden and had an attendant to help him. When we went to his room, he was lying on his bed and being almost deaf, the attendant shouted in his ear our names and that we had come to meet him. He suddenly seemed to understand and stirred and then with great effort sat up and even tried to stand up to meet us. The pathos of the moment was not lost and we left teary-eyed but with a sense of great satisfaction.

During a visit to the leper colony in Ludhiana, I had noted that there were a number of small children who were totally free from the disease but were, in a sense, condemned to live, ostracised by society in the leper colony. I pondered on what we could do to improve the plight of these unfortunate children. I asked a few of the inmates if they would be agreeable to have their children leave the colony and be provided an opportunity to live in an open society. The sense of their response was definitely positive. We, therefore, went ahead to plan our second institution, a home for the healthy children of parents afflicted with leprosy. A hostel was built just next to the Senior Citizens Home and we had about 80 children, ranging from five years to near adults who moved into the hostel. Simultaneously, arrangements were made for their education. The senior citizens living next door were happy to accept our suggestion to be their foster parents. It was a mutually happy arrangement to see the two sections sitting together out in the lawn as one big happy family. The parents of one of the older children, a girl who was over eighteen, were very keen to get her married. We were able to find a suitable groom for her with a stable and credible family background. The wedding took place at the Senior Citizens Home complex and Chief Minister Darbara Singh was present to bless the newlyweds.

Ludhiana has a number of educational institutions apart from the well-known Punjab Agriculture University. It has specialised medical and engineering colleges in addition to the normal general institutions.

What appeared to be lacking was an institution to meet the special needs of challenged children. We, therefore, decided to set up another Red Cross institution to meet the needs of deaf and dumb children. A vocational training centre was set up in the same complex to cater to such children, especially from low income groups. The encouraging response bore testimony to the pressing need for such a facility. The complex then looked complete with the Senior Citizens Home and the hostel on one side and the vocational training school on the other, each fostering the other.

One of the major activities of the Red Cross Society was organising blood donation camps and it was almost customary that to encourage donors, the Deputy Commissioner and his wife would be the first to donate blood. We had organised such camps periodically but often non-availability of blood of a particular type remained a recurring problem. There was no central facility in the district or in the state which could meet such contingencies. We, therefore, decided to set up a Blood Bank in Ludhiana which would not only meet the needs of the district but the whole state. The Blood Bank was set up next to the Red Cross Bhawan and soon after its inauguration by the Chief Minister, it fulfilled the much felt need in the state.

Sometimes a small act can transform a person's life completely, as we witnessed when one day a young polio victim on a skateboard attempted to enter the Deputy Commissioner's residence. He was abruptly stopped by the armed security at the gate. Just then Madhu was driving in and she witnessed the incident. She asked the security guards to let the person in and came to me to check whether we could give some assistance from the Red Cross Society. We first thought of a financial donation but then realised that that would bring him only temporary relief. We, therefore, decided that Red Cross would set up a booth in the civil courts compound for him to sell soft drinks. Lalji, as was his name, started his little business in real earnest. In course of time, he set up an STD phone facility in the booth. For years Lalji would call us, when we were in Delhi and also after we moved to Bangkok, to greet us every Diwali and New Year. When we visited Ludhiana years later, we went to Lalji's booth. His business was doing well and he had got married and had two schoolgoing children. On our arrival, he immediately shut down his booth and called his family to meet us. It was a delightful moment to see how Lalji's life had transformed by just a small gesture.

There are also unpleasant incidents that one has at times to deal with. For me foremost was one involving a so-called scribe indulging in 'yellow journalism'. He printed a two-page weekly paper, not more than 200 copies, and distributed them free. He exploited his pseudo status as a journalist to gain favours from the district administration, in particular getting permits for cement on a regular basis. Cement was in very short supply then and the district administration had to issue permits for people to buy it at controlled prices. In the beginning, I sanctioned him cement a few times which was ostensibly for repairing his house. When repeated requests were made, I checked his credentials and was informed by my office that he had been a habitual applicant for cement and my predecessors had accommodated him because of his nuisance value. The next time he applied, I enquired the reason for his repeated requests for cement and he gave his standard response that it was for repairing his house. I deputed a Magistrate to inspect his house before sanctioning any more cement. As suspected, the Magistrate verified that no such repairs had been or were being carried out. He had been getting cement on a regular basis and selling it on the black market at a premium, which in those days was quite high. After the supply of cement was stopped to him, he went on a tirade against me and my wife in his paper. Baseless allegations and insinuations were made, aspersions were cast on our moral character and integrity. Many from the public approached me not to tolerate this blackmailing and to take some stern action against him.

I chose to write to the government drawing its attention to the matter and suggested that the government either order an enquiry against me or take action to withdraw his licence. However, before the government could decide on action to be taken, the recalcitrant journalist was accosted by some people and was beaten up. He alleged that I was behind that attack on him. It was definitely not my way of handling such a situation. Apparently, he owed a lot of money to people and since his income from cement black marketing stopped, he was unable to repay and that probably led to the violence against him. He, however, chose to press charges against me at the Press Council of India, then headed by Justice A.N. Grover. In the very first hearing, the charges against me were dropped and the complainant was admonished for the malicious charge.

There are also times when a Deputy Commissioner has to perform certain functions for good public relations. Ludhiana city has a very large Jain community which has contributed immensely to its economic growth and welfare of the people. Among them were some of the larger industrial houses like Hero and Oswal. There was a labour strike in Hero Cycles which was threatening to turn violent. This was a crucial time for the company as it was then in the process of negotiating collaboration with Honda of Japan. The company had declared a lockout and when I, accompanied by police, arrived there, a large number of strikers were at the locked main gate threatening to break it down. We met the agitating labour leaders and were able to convince them that the management would sympathetically consider their demands provided they called off the strike.

In the case of Oswal's Vardhman Spinning Mills, there was actual violence among different factions of the labour union and a few had lost their lives. When we arrived there, the police took into custody the rival labour leaders and this immediate intervention of the administration defused the situation and brought the matter under control. Dealing with such incidents is part and parcel of the administrative machinery in a district. What was unusual and totally unexpected was taking part in the cremation of a Jain sadhvi. A very senior and revered Jain sadhvi passed away in Ludhiana. Her cremation was held in the sports stadium in order to accommodate the hundreds of thousands of her followers from all over the country, who were expected to attend the funeral. A delegation of prominent members of the Jain community came and requested me to participate in the funeral and to light the pyre. It is customary in the Jain community when the final rites of a revered monk are to be conducted, bids are invited and people respond in large numbers to participate. Understanding the sentiment involved and its significance before the massive Jain community, I agreed to do so. As I was told years later, memory of that gesture remains deeply etched in the hearts of the Jain community.

We stayed in Ludhiana for over three years and our daughters, Ravina and Aushima were still in their infancy. Ravina had started going to a kindergarten school and seemed to enjoy it, especially when she participated in a fancy dress event as a 'flower girl'. A local artist made a painting of her which adorned our walls for many years. Aushima was just beginning to walk and was a very strong and active child and so needed close watching. Her love for dogs was already evident amidst our pet dogs. She was happiest carrying the newly born pups, even when she could barely walk. As Madhu was also very busy with Red Cross work, we restrained our social life so that we could spend time with the children in the evenings. Apart from a few old school friends who lived in or near Ludhiana, we made some good friends, and some have remained friends even today. Among them were Mukesh and Poonam Verma, who lived just across from us, and the Bector family which from a modest beginning with a catering outlet in the Red Cross Bhavan have now emerged as a nationally famous enterprise—Cremica.

Then there was a golf playing couple, Lali and Ranjit Grewal, a former national golfer, so I could get an occasional game of golf over a weekend, either at the Punjab Agriculture University or in Phillaur. The Services Club was located just next to my residence so was very easily accessible through a private side entrance. I was into playing squash those days but there was no squash court in the club. I had a squash court constructed there and it soon became a very popular sport. Having been an athlete, I thought I could still play and stretch with the same ease and gusto, only to tear my leg muscles twice and having to be on crutches the second time. That ended days of my playing squash. I have since then stuck to golf.

In early 1983, our family suffered a terrible tragedy. Madhu's elder brother, Kavi, passed away at the young age of 29. The family was totally devastated. Madhu's parents were then living in Delhi so we started thinking of shifting to Delhi to be with them. I conveyed my request to the government to be sent on deputation to the Government of India. Having explained the situation to the Chief Minister, he reluctantly agreed to have my name forwarded to the Government of India. Few months later, I received confirmation that the Ministry of Commerce had selected me to join as Director. *The Tribune* newspaper carried the news of my appointment and so it became public knowledge almost immediately. The spate of farewell parties started as is customary. What was totally unexpected was the invitation by Akali leaders to honour me in Gurdwara Kalgidhar. They insisted that my wife must also be present because the honour they were going to bestow on me was an unprecedented gesture by them to any outgoing Deputy Commissioner. We were received at the gurdwara by the local senior leaders and Akali MLAs in the presence of a large gathering. It was announced that they were honouring me with seven *saropas* (scarf and *kirpan*) which was unprecedented, in appreciation of my non-partisan and effective performance as Deputy Commissioner, because of which, Ludhiana district had remained peaceful and incident-free throughout the turbulent period in Punjab.

On the day of departure, there were a large number of people from the city and other parts of the district to bid us farewell. They insisted on pushing our car till we got to the main road. It was their way of saying 'bon voyage'. We left with a sense of satisfaction over a very fulfilling tenure as Deputy Commissioner, but also with a touch of sadness that we were leaving behind the Red Cross institutions, which had become so much a part of our life.

9

Punjab to Delhi

Life is not a continuum of pleasant choices,
but of inevitable problems that call for strength,
determination, and hard work.

—Indian proverb

I arrived at the Union Commerce Ministry and went directly to meet the Commerce Secretary, the affable Abid Hussain. Extending a warm welcome, the first thing he said was, 'Babu, enjoy your work'. *Babu* was his usual way of addressing anyone and yet it appeared to have a personal undertone to it. From that moment I felt that with a boss like him, I was definitely going to enjoy working in that Ministry, and henceforth, 'enjoy your work' became my mantra whenever I welcomed a newcomer.

I then met T.S.R. Subramanian (TSR), who was Joint Secretary, Administration, and later rose to become Cabinet Secretary. He informed me of the work allocated to me—trade development with East Asia, export promotion of chemicals and allied products, and United Nations ESCAP. It was an ideal mix of territorial charge, commodity export promotion and an international organisation. I could understand the territorial and commodity charges but had never heard of ESCAP. Hence, one of the first things I did back in my room was to check what ESCAP was. Little did I know then what an important role that organisation would play in my future.

ESCAP, the acronym for the Economic and Social Commission for Asia and the Pacific, is one of the five regional commissions set up by the United Nations after the Second World War to assist developing countries in their economic and social development. In terms of its constituency, it is the largest and most diverse of the five regional commissions covering almost 60 countries from Turkey in the West to Japan in the East and from the then Soviet Union in the North to New Zealand and South Pacific Island countries. Abid Hussain had worked in ESCAP and so he attached considerable importance to it. The territorial charge included all countries east of India but excluding the South Asian neighbours. The commodity charge involved working with three export promotion councils dealing with chemicals, pharmaceuticals, chemical allied products and plastics, namely CHEMEXIL, CAPEXIL and PLEXCONCIL. It appeared to be a very interesting mix of work and most importantly, I had been given independent charge as Director, reporting directly to the Commerce Secretary.

We settled in very quickly as we were lucky to be allotted government accommodation in Rabindra Nagar in central Delhi, near the well-known Khan Market. Madhu got down to refurbishing the ground floor two-bedroom apartment. Ravina was admitted to Junior Modern

School, and Aushima started attending a kindergarten school, Tiny Tots, both very conveniently near Khan Market. My office in Udyog Bhawan was just a 10-minute drive from home, and the Delhi Golf Club just five minutes away.

My immediate preoccupation in the ministry was to prepare for a regional meeting Commerce Minister V.P. Singh, who later on became the Prime Minister, was to have with Commercial Counsellors from Indian Embassies in the East Asian countries in Hong Kong. The meeting was just about two months away and so preparatory work had to start immediately. The importance of this meeting was further enhanced as it included a major country, Japan, and two potentially important trading countries, China and South Korea. A comprehensive brief was to be prepared with inputs from the missions, which became a very valuable learning exercise for me. As it was my first meeting overseas and that too presided over by the Minister, I was naturally nervous. Fortunately, V.P. Singh was happy with the brief and I was impressed that he had read it thoroughly. The meeting went off to the satisfaction of the Minister and instilled a lot of confidence in me. I felt I was now ready to handle whatever came my way.

My first experience with ESCAP was a few months later. As the Indian delegate, I was to attend a meeting of the ESCAP Special Body for Landlocked Countries, which primarily addressed the concerns of the then five landlocked countries: Afghanistan, Bhutan, Nepal, Lao PDR, and Mongolia vis-à-vis their corresponding transit countries: India, Pakistan, China and Thailand. I was warned that during the previous meeting attended by my predecessor, very contentious and acrimonious exchanges had taken place between the Indian and Nepalese delegations over the transit facilities being provided by India to Nepal. India and Nepal have a bilateral trade and transit treaty and matters, which normally should be addressed in the bilateral forum, were sought to be raised by Nepal in a multilateral forum, much to the chagrin of the Indian delegation. Similarly, other landlocked countries expressed dissatisfaction over the transit facilities available to them, but not so vociferously.

In order to avoid the acrimony of earlier meetings, I thought of bringing a strategic shift in the focus of discussion at the meeting. The United Nations resolution which had created the Special Body had also proposed the establishment of a Special Fund to assist landlocked countries. Hitherto, no attention had been paid to the creation of this Fund. The principal donors were expected to be the developed countries. Thus, in the meeting, in my opening statement, I said that in this region all the transit countries were also developing countries and, therefore, they too faced severe resource constraints in extending concessions to their landlocked neighbours. Hence, they were doing whatever they could within the framework of bilateral treaties to meet the needs of the landlocked countries. Unfortunately, the developed countries had not fulfilled their commitment in establishing the Special Fund and should, therefore, be called upon to do so. All the landlocked and other transit countries, taking my cue, targeted the developed countries in their interventions as one united group. There were, thus, no acrimonious exchanges between India and Nepal. After the meeting, S.A.M.S. Kibria, Executive Secretary of ESCAP, told me he had been apprehensive that the acrimony of the previous meeting would be repeated and thanked me for the constructive approach I had taken in steering the meeting to a meaningful conclusion.

During a periodic review meeting taken by the Commerce Secretary, it was observed that India's trade with China was minuscule, considering the size of the two economies. After the 1962 conflict there had been no attempt by either government to promote bilateral trade in order to realise the existing huge potential. We decided to explore the possibility of establishing some form of government-to-government understanding so that a conscious effort could be made to develop two-way trade. India's Ambassador to China, A.P. Venkateswaran (Venky), who subsequently became Foreign Secretary, confirmed that China would respond positively to such an initiative. We, therefore, started working on a Trade Protocol between the two governments, targeting a level of two-way trade of just US$1 billion in three years, bearing testimony to the hitherto very low level of trade. After a series of negotiations in Beijing and Delhi, we had the Protocol ready for signatures by the two governments.

Commerce Secretary Abid Hussain led the delegation to China, which included Vinod Dikshit from the Department of Economic Affairs, Ministry of Finance, (husband of Sheila Dikshit who served as Delhi Chief Minister for three terms), Mani Shankar Aiyar, Joint Secretary, Ministry of External Affairs, and from the Commerce Ministry, Deepak Nayyar, Economic Adviser and I. The event was accorded very high priority by the Chinese government, as was evident from the high profile status the visit was accorded and the extravagant hospitality extended. We stayed at the Beijing Hotel, a state-owned hotel, as there were no five star hotels then. At that time, the only high-rise building was the China International Trust Investment Corporation building. There were very few cars visible on the roads as the common mode of transport was buses or bicycles.

Just a day before the signing of the Trade Protocol document, we were informed that the Chinese government wanted to also sign a Chinese translation of the Protocol. As we had no option, we agreed but felt that on the basis of reciprocity, we should also have a Hindi translation signed. As we did not have a Hindi copy ready, Abid Hussain asked us to prepare one overnight. Fortunately, both Vinod and Deepak were fluent in Hindi and well equipped to undertake the task of translation but they needed an English-Hindi dictionary to translate the more technical terms and to ensure the correctness of the official language. The Indian Embassy did not have such a dictionary and neither was it available in the market. The Embassy was finally able to locate one with the Chinese Radio Station, which was loaned to us and we could prepare a Hindi translation of the Protocol overnight.

The Trade Protocol was signed by the Commerce Secretary and the Chinese Vice-Minister on 15 August 1984, India's Independence Day. Abid Hussain was visibly emotional, given the huge significance of the event as it was the first agreement between the two governments after the 1962 conflict. The significance of the event to the Chinese could be gauged by the extraordinary importance given to our delegation. After the signing, our delegation was received by the Vice-Chairman of the Communist Party in the Great Hall of the People. He was visibly moved by Abid's eloquence, as was evident from his repeated nodding of the head in approval and at times, applauding, as Abid's statements were interpreted to him.

After conclusion of the official work in Beijing, the delegation was taken to Shanghai as guests of the Chinese government. We stayed at the Jin Jiang Hotel, which had become famous after US President Richard Nixon had stayed there. Walking along the 'Bund', I saw a long queue leading into a building that extended to the road. Out of curiosity, I went to check and found it was a queue outside a cinema hall screening a Hindi movie! I was surprised to find out that Hindi movies were extremely popular in China. Later, when I visited some shops, they were listening to Indian 'filmi' songs, relayed by the radio station in Hong Kong. From Shanghai we were taken to the Shenzhen, the special economic zone which was then at the planning stage. There was just the project office and Shenzhen was still on the drawing board. Heavy machinery could be seen levelling the land. The next time I visited Shenzhen, just a few years later, it had unbelievably developed to look almost like Hong Kong.

In June 1984, Operation Blue Star had taken place in which Bhindranwale was killed. Following that, tension had gripped the country, particularly in Punjab. The Akalis were incensed but the more militant sections were screaming for revenge. On 31 October 1984, Prime Minister Indira Gandhi was assassinated by her own security guards. Reportedly, in the wake of Operation Blue Star, the Prime Minister had been advised on withdrawing all the Sikh security guards but she had declined as she felt it would not look good to the people. If that indeed were true, it is baffling why she was ever consulted. The cardinal rule in security is never to consult the person being secured as security arrangements must depend on threat perception. Even if the Prime Minister were not consulted, the serious threat perception should have warranted the replacement of all Sikh security personnel with non-Sikhs, and in order not to offend sensibility of the community which has been at the forefront of patriotism, they could have been camouflaged as Sikhs. I remain bewildered why the security establishment never thought of this. I cannot help but conjecture as to what might have been the outcome if we had succeeded in bringing about a rapprochement between the Congress and the Akalis.

Among the large number of world leaders, who gathered in Delhi to pay their last respects to Indira Gandhi, was Imelda Marcos, wife of Philippine President Ferdinand Marcos. We met one evening when a common friend brought her over to my father-in-law's home. In the course of our conversation, I informed her that I was in charge of bilateral trade with the Philippines and she expressed keen interest in developing economic relations with India, and in particular, learning from India's experience in the development of small and medium enterprises. She asked me to meet her whenever I visited Manila.

A few months later, I was in Manila for our annual bilateral trade discussions. I requested Ambassador Ramesh Mulye if the Embassy could coordinate with the office of Imelda Marcos for an appointment. He was initially reticent, knowing how difficult it was to meet her. He was also sceptical as he had not been able to get an appointment himself since he assumed charge as Ambassador some months back. Hence, he thought, where was the possibility of a Director level officer meeting her? On my insistence, he reluctantly agreed to have the message conveyed. To his surprise, a confirmation came within a few hours for a meeting the next morning and he excitedly called me adding that he would accompany me to the meeting. Much to our surprise, there were press and TV reporters present to cover the meeting. We spent a good hour with Imelda Marcos and though it was an informal meeting, it appeared to be a productive start for the Embassy to promote cooperation between the two countries, especially in the development of small and medium enterprises that she reiterated at the meeting. The next morning, the *Manila Times* carried a front page report with a photograph of my meeting with Imelda Marcos.

Prem Kumar had taken over as Commerce Secretary, replacing Abid Hussain after his superannuation. I was promoted as Joint Secretary, initially holding the same charge but later also South Asia, including Iran as well as the Administration Branch. It was the heaviest allocation among the Joint Secretaries. That notwithstanding, I never stayed late evening in the office and neither did I leave office with any work pending. As a matter of principle, I never carried work home and never carried home to work. I would normally clear a lot of my file work, most of it relating to administration matters, quite undisturbed during the lunch break. I was not part of any of the two main lunch groups in the Ministry which met over extended lunch breaks, the main one in the Additional Secretary's office discussing astrology and the other discussing politics. I usually took my lunch break whenever I felt I had 15 minutes to spare.

With the major trading countries, India had institutionalized mechanisms for annual meetings, such as Joint Commissions, the level of representation depending on the importance of the country. Bilateral meetings would normally take place alternately in the capitals of the two countries. In the East Asia region, Japan was the only country with which the Joint Commission was at the level of the Commerce Secretary, and for the others, principal among them being Australia, South Korea, Indonesia, Malaysia, Singapore and Thailand, I led the Indian delegation. Trade with Malaysia needed special attention as the bilateral trade was heavily one-sided, in favour of Malaysia.

India was importing about one million tons of palm oil annually which was about 25 per cent of Malaysia's total annual exports of four million tons. The quantity of import of 'Bombay onions' by Malaysia, though significant, was negligible in comparison. Past attempts to get Malaysia to expand its imports from India in order to bring greater balance in the two-way trade had proved futile. We decided to leverage our import power to get a more meaningful response from the Malaysian government. To get the message across and get their serious attention, for the first time we bought 10,000 tons of palm oil from Indonesia. As expected, that hit the newspaper headlines in Malaysia and it had the desired effect. At a special meeting in Kuala Lumpur, the Malaysian Ministers of Finance, Natural Resources and Trade were present and we worked out a special arrangement involving the establishment of an Evidence Account, to enable Indian companies to get infrastructure development projects in Malaysia.

Malaysian Finance Minister Daim Zainuddin, who I had got to know quite well in the course of these negotiations, and on one trip, he had taken me to the famous Genting Island, subsequently visited India in 1988 and concluded the bilateral agreement establishing the Evidence Account and we parted on very friendly terms. Subsequently, projects were earmarked for allotment to Indian companies including development of Ipoh airport, construction of a national highway and establishing a tool room training centre.

The leveraging of import power and how to use it strategically can be very effective in bilateral trade relations. China had been doing it, importing at what they called 'friendship price' even items they might themselves be exporting and, in return, extracting market access for their exports. China had been buying rice from Myanmar at a 'friendship price' and had in return exporting plant and machinery for milling paddy. We were approached by Myanmar to annually import 20,000 tons of rice and, in return, they were willing to give us market access for passenger and goods transport vehicles. In addition, they would buy jute from India against the export of the rice.

I submitted a proposal, highlighting the positives from a strategic import of a quantity of rice which would not impact negatively on the domestic market, also emphasizing that the quality of imported rice would be preferred by consumers in the North-Eastern states which, very importantly, would save cost of transporting rice by rail from the more distant states like Haryana and Punjab. Additionally, there was the imperative need to stave off the growing Chinese influence in our immediate neighbourhood. The proposal was sent to various Ministries, including the Department of Food in the Ministry of Agriculture. They opposed the proposal on the ground that India had become self-sufficient in food production and so there was no need to import the rice. It was unfortunate that we could not capitalize on that opportunity because of the narrow-minded stand taken by a Ministry and its failure to take a more holistic view, especially when it involved our neighbourhood.

In 1985, New Zealand decided to reopen its mission in Delhi after a gap of many years and they did it with a masterstroke by appointing Sir Edmund Hillary as their High Commissioner. With someone who was a household name in India, the mission immediately came into prominence. It was a small mission and the Commercial Counsellor was young and inexperienced, so the High Commissioner was directly involved in all discussions on bilateral trade. The trade expansion prospects were very limited with India already importing wool tops and New Zealand mainly trying to push export of timber pallets. The High Commissioner's insistence on my visiting New Zealand never materialized. We, however, met socially quite often and Madhu and I spent many a memorable evening with Sir Edmund Hillary and Lady June at their residence.

Iran was an important trading partner given India's dependence on Iranian crude oil. There were some long pending issues with Iran revolving around their failure to fulfil past commitments to imports from India. Some of these items had been custom made for Iran and could not, therefore, easily find alternate markets. Our Foreign Ministry and Mission in Tehran had been pressing Iran to fulfil its commitments. We were told that at the forthcoming visit of the Iranian delegation, coming to negotiate new oil contracts, the outstanding issues would also be addressed. Prem Kumar, Commerce Secretary, had in my presence called the Secretary, Economic Relations (ER) in the Foreign Ministry and got his assurance that the Iranian delegation was coming prepared to fulfil all outstanding commitments. When we met the Iranian delegation, I proposed that before we discussed oil purchases, we needed to address the outstanding issue of unfulfilled contracts. The delegation appeared disinclined in spite of my assertion that our Foreign Ministry had conveyed to us the delegation's readiness to do so. As they were showing no flexibility, we adjourned the discussions to give them time to reflect.

The Iranian Ambassador contacted Secretary (ER) to complain against my 'rigid' stand. The Secretary (ER) called me and rebuked me, to which I reacted with the question as to whose side was he on. I said he should have pressed the Iranian Ambassador to fulfil their commitments as per the assurance given to him, rather than to take their side. Having spoken to a Secretary so bluntly, I immediately went to the Commerce Secretary's room to apprise him and while doing so, the Secretary (ER) called to complain about my stand. The Commerce Secretary retorted that my position was fully consistent with the brief given to us by the Foreign Ministry and reminded the Secretary (ER) that he had personally confirmed that over the telephone. The discussions then proceeded on a more acceptable track and we were able to sort out most of the outstanding issues before committing ourselves to future purchases of Iranian crude.

That was not the only time I appeared to be in confrontation with a Secretary level officer in the Central government. The Commerce Secretary deputed me to attend, on his behalf, a meeting of the Committee of Secretaries, which is chaired by the Cabinet Secretary, the senior-most civil servant in the country. The meeting's agenda included a proposal, mooted by the Ministry of Chemicals, to grant cash compensatory support (CCS) on the export of a chemical product, and since I was dealing with the chemicals sector, it seemed normal that the Commerce Secretary should depute me to attend the meeting. CCS is granted on items for export to neutralize the impact of local taxes and levies in order to make the item more competitive in the international market and thereby realize more fully the item's potential for export on a sustained basis. The CCS Committee in the Commerce Ministry examines proposals and decides whether an item is eligible for CCS and if so, what percentage of CCS should be granted, the ceiling being 20 per cent. However, in this case CCS was sought to be given, circumventing the normal procedure through an unprecedented decision in a meeting of the Committee of Secretaries.

In preparation for the meeting, I had done due diligence and had consulted the relevant council, CHEMEXCIL. It was a chemical item manufactured by Reliance, a powerful private sector company that wielded considerable influence in government circles, and hence it was the applicant for CCS. When the agenda item was introduced by the Secretary Chemicals, strongly supporting the grant of CCS, the Cabinet Secretary turned to me to comment on the proposal. I responded that the item was not eligible for CCS as it appeared to be a one-time export and there was no exportable surplus to expect sustained exports. Further, the applicant company had already concluded a contract with a Chinese importer so it was not a case of making the item competitive for export but, in fact, it was giving undue benefit ex post facto. I further added that as there is a set procedure for processing such applications based on objective criteria in the CCS Committee, the Committee of Secretaries meeting was not the forum for deciding such cases.

The Secretary Chemicals looked visibly agitated and pressed for at least a decision in principle to grant CCS of 20 per cent, which is the maximum, pending the processing in the CCS Committee. I opposed that too, as it would amount to pre-empting the normal process and emphasized that the Committee of Secretaries could not impose such a decision on the CCS Committee. Summing up the discussion, the Cabinet Secretary said that the Commerce Ministry should process the proposal on fast track and communicate its decision to his office. As the processing of the case could be initiated only on the submission of proper data representative of the industry, I requested that the Ministry of Chemicals advise the applicant company to submit credible data expeditiously. On return to office, I immediately briefed the Commerce Secretary of what had transpired in the meeting. He smiled and said he was aware something like that would happen and he wanted to see how I would handle it.

A delegation of the applicant company, Reliance, met me a few days later and assured the submission of credible and industry representative data. The data eventually submitted by them was largely fictitious and obviously so, as industrial data for that single item was not readily available. What was alarming was that almost on a daily basis, I was visited in the evening by a Joint Secretary level officer from the Cabinet Secretariat to check with me the progress and to report back. At the end, all attempts to grant undue CCS to Reliance were thwarted and the integrity of the policy remained intact.

The Treaty of Trade and Transit, which was signed with Nepal on 11 September 1960, was due for renewal. As usual, with neighbouring countries, political considerations invariably underpin trade negotiations and we had been extending concessions to Nepal without insisting on full reciprocity. Nepal was seeking not just renewal of trade concessions already extended to it but further concessions and relaxation of rules of origin as well as greater transit facilities at the seaport in Kolkata.

We were concerned about Nepal's rigid position on extending some reciprocity in matters of concern to us. An Indian company, Wimco, had invested in a matchstick manufacturing plant in Nepal, which was ordered to be closed down by its government. In response to the sudden closure ordered by the Nepalese government, on the ground that it had resulted in large-scale deforestation, Wimco had submitted a proposal to undertake reforestation in the vicinity of the factory. We raised the matter with the Nepalese government but it was not willing to relent. I then asked them to at least give us an assurance that before issuing any new licence for a similar industry, the first option would be given to Wimco to reopen its unit. They refused to give any such assurance which created suspicion whether the closure of the Indian venture was actually because of concern about deforestation or was it due to some external political pressure from a third country. This was one among other instances of Nepal showing its unwillingness to extend cooperation and reciprocity. This prompted us to take a slightly harder line in our forthcoming negotiations on the renewal of the bilateral treaty when our delegation led by the Commerce Secretary visited Nepal.

The negotiations, as expected, were difficult as we unequivocally conveyed our unwillingness to extend unilateral concessions giving market access to exports from Nepal, as we had done in the past almost on a non-reciprocal basis. However, when the minutes, usually prepared by the host country, were tabled for signatures, they were contrary to the facts, reflecting that we had conceded several concessions. This unprecedented situation was extremely embarrassing as the minutes had to be revised extensively. As the Commerce Secretary had to return to Delhi, I had to cancel my departure and stay on till we had a mutually agreed document for signatures. The final document was given to me as I was at the departure lounge at the airport and it was signed after several sentences that still did not accurately reflect our discussions were redacted.

Ironically, during the same trip, Nepal was facing a severe shortage of sugar. With the approaching Dussehra festival, which is one of their biggest festivals, the demand for sugar increased manifold. Hence, it was almost a crisis situation. On the sidelines of the meeting, we were asked to extend assistance on an emergency basis. We were able to divert a shipment on the high seas to Kolkata port for transhipment to Nepal. Hence, whatever unhappiness that might have been generated due to our principled stand ended with a sugar coating!

We faced a somewhat similar situation with Bangladesh, which expected non-reciprocal concessions from India. In my meeting with their Commerce Secretary, he lamented the heavily skewed trade in India's favour. In response, I explained that Bangladesh was pushing exports mainly of Hilsa fish and jamdani sarees. The quantity of the fish available for export was limited and the market in India, too, was small, mainly to West Bengal. The demand for jamdani sarees in India was also very limited. Import of jute products on a large scale was not feasible as the jute industry in India would be adversely affected. On the other hand, Bangladesh could export large volume of newsprint and natural gas for which India was a huge market. So I queried why they were reluctant to export these items. The Bangladesh Commerce Secretary could give me no cogent explanation beyond a wry smile and I could only assume that the reason against deeper economic integration must be political.

India's trade with South Korea too was well below its potential, so it became a focus of special attention. Both countries were members of a regional preferential trade agreement, called the Bangkok Agreement. The other members were Bangladesh, Sri Lanka and Lao PDR. The Agreement was signed in Bangkok in 1976, hence the name. Though a signatory to the Agreement, Thailand never ratified it and remained a non-member, but the name continued. The potential of the Agreement to expand trade was, therefore, limited by its small membership. It, however, provided a framework for negotiating exchange of tariff concessions between India and South Korea. We accordingly pushed for a new round of trade negotiations, to which South Korea eventually agreed and hosted the Second Round of Trade Negotiations, and the list of items enjoying tariff concessions was expanded substantially. Later when I was working in ESCAP, I was able to get China to also join the Agreement which added substantially to its significance as a regional trade agreement. Subsequently, the Agreement also went through a name change and became the Asia-Pacific Trade Agreement (APTA), with ESCAP continuing to be the secretariat.

Japan was India's most important trading partner in the Asia-Pacific region. The trade balance was heavily weighted in favour of Japan, and understandably so. The Joint Trade Commission meetings were at the level of the Commerce Secretary with Japan Deputy Minister, Foreign Affairs, as his counterpart. The first meeting of the Joint Trade Commission that I attended was in Delhi and the Japanese delegation was led by Deputy Minister Hiroshi Kitamura. Given the profile of the two-way trade, we were not seeking to achieve balanced trade but dynamic equilibrium, whereby there is growth in trade on both sides. A tangible outcome of these meetings was an agreement by Japan to host an exhibition of Indian light engineering goods, to be organized by the Japan External Trade Organization (JETRO) in Tokyo. It was indeed a positive development in our effort to diversify India's exports to value-added manufactured goods. For me personally, having been invited by JETRO as the Chief Guest, it was a memorable experience.

Kitamura had worked in the Japanese Embassy in Delhi in the early 1960s and reminiscing about his stay in India, he told me about the unforgettable experience he had at the Delhi Golf Club. He was a regular at the club and one day playing the 16th hole, which has a sharp dogleg to the right, he hit what seemed a good second shot and so was sure that his ball was on the green. However, when he came around the bend, he could not see his ball on the green, only to find it in the hole. His forecaddie told him that a monkey, and in those days monkeys were in abundance on the course, had picked up his ball and had dropped it in the hole! After some argument among his fellow golfers, especially as there was no precedent, he was eventually given a birdie on that hole. On his return to Japan, Kitamura sent me a letter of appreciation which I would like to quote here as Japanese officials by their very nature tend to be very reserved in expressing such sentiments.

> Thank you very much for your personal kindness and thoughtfulness which made my recent visit to India most pleasant and memorable. I appreciated your help profoundly.
>
> I should also like to take this opportunity to commend your initiative of keeping close contact with Japan. Your visit to Japan last month was particularly timely as it was made just before our Trade Talks.
>
> *P.S. I deeply appreciate your cordial welcome and farewell at the airport at such odd hours of a day.*

On another occasion, I was in Tokyo, just over a month before Prime Minister Rajiv Gandhi's state visit to Japan. Discussions were held with officers from the Foreign Ministry as well as the Ministry of International Trade and Industry (MITI), covering some of the issues that would come up for discussion during the Prime Minister's visit. Our discussions carried on till late evening followed by dinner. The hosts indicated that they were going back to office after dinner to continue to prepare for the Prime Minister's visit. I remarked that the visit was still more than a month away, only to learn that those officers had been burning midnight oil for the last three months, preparing for the visit. In the more informal setting, that led to a discussion on our comparative lifestyles as senior government officers. It was a revelation that in a developed country like Japan, life for our counterparts was comparatively far more taxing and stressful, as it was bereft of regular recreation time, including with family. They appeared envious when I said that I could get time for recreation (golf) regularly and spend adequate time with my family, primarily because of easy accessibility to place of work and recreational facilities. My office was about 10 minutes away and the golf course just five minutes away from my home, something inconceivable in Tokyo.

In pursuance of Prime Minister Rajiv Gandhi's 'Look East' policy, he visited several countries in the region. Among them was Vietnam, a country with which India had longstanding political and economic ties. The visit was viewed as highly successful in further cementing bilateral relations and very significantly, Vietnam had offered India offshore blocks for oil exploration. However, a few months later, there was a sudden transfer of power by the ruling government to a younger leadership in Vietnam. That change was a matter of great concern to our government, as the momentum generated during the Prime Minister's visit, might dissipate.

The Prime Minister, therefore, decided to send a high-level delegation to establish contact with the new government. Accordingly, a delegation, led by N.D. Tiwari, who was then Commerce Minister, and including Natwar Singh, Minister of State, Foreign Affairs; Bhram Dutt, Minister of State, Petroleum; B.K. Gadhvi, Minister of State, Finance; and Col S.P. Wahi, Chairman ONGC, was sent. H.C.S. Dhody, Joint Secretary, Ministry of Foreign Affairs, and I were the two officials accompanying the ministerial delegation.

The visit achieved its purpose in renewing the agreements reached during the Prime Minister's visit. However, the multi-ministerial composition of the delegation did present complications during the negotiations. There seemed to be attempts at times by Natwar Singh to take control of the discussions and thus project himself as leader of the delegation. Also evident was the lack of experience and finesse demonstrated by the other two Ministers in conducting international diplomacy and negotiations. The Vietnamese are fiercely independent people as they have shown against the more powerful adversaries. Hence, to be reminded in a patronizing tone the bilateral assistance and credits given by India in the past, especially when dealing with the new generation of leadership, could have created an embarrassing situation were it not for timely clarifications offered by the accompanying officials.

Trade with the Democratic People's Republic of Korea (North Korea) was a difficult proposition, mainly because of difficulty in communication and the opaque role played by intermediaries in Hong Kong. India was making significant imports of items like railway rolling stock and cement, which made North Korea an important trading partner. Our exports were mainly commodities and food grains. As was customary with our major trading partners, we had annual bilateral trade negotiations alternately in Delhi and Pyongyang. On my first visit to Pyongyang as leader of the Indian delegation, I was shocked how isolated the country was and how cut-off people were from the rest of the world. As was customary, immediately on arrival, one had to first pay respects to a statue of its great leader, Kim II-sung. India was the only non-socialist country with an Embassy there and it was perhaps the most difficult posting for any diplomat. The socialist countries had a club but India was not a member, so Indian diplomats had no access to any recreational facility.

Japan had a one-man office in the only hotel where we stayed. His role was primarily to study the speeches of the Great Leader and advise Tokyo accordingly. The drivers and security personnel, provided by the North Korean government, maintained a constant vigil on the movement of diplomatic staff and kept surveillance over any interaction with the local people which was forbidden. Even we, as an official foreign delegation, could not step out of the hotel unescorted. An interesting visit was that to the Children's Palace, a large imposing building. Children were brought there after school to be taught fine arts like musical instruments, dancing, painting, etc., depending upon their aptitude. What struck me more was that the brightest children were selected for political indoctrination. I travelled to North Korea several times after that, both while in government and at the United Nations, and saw little, if any, change. Perhaps, the most notable change in subsequent visits was to first go to the mausoleum, and not the statue, to pay respects to the body of the Great Leader.

Trade with Pakistan remained minuscule given the strained political relations. Pakistan had consistently refused to give India MFN (Most Favoured Nation) status although it was obliged to do so as member of GATT/WTO. Their High Commissioner to India, Humayun

Khan, happened to come from the same alma mater, Bishop Cotton School, Shimla, having left prematurely, when a group left mid-year to join their families in the newly created Pakistan at the time of the Partition. We, therefore, enjoyed great camaraderie but it could never get translated to something meaningful in our official relations. I questioned him on not extending MFN status to India and his response was that this was in retaliation to India's import tariffs being very high on items Pakistan could export to India. He chose to make this fallacious argument knowing fully well that the Indian import tariff regime was of universal application and not discriminatory to Pakistan. He informed me that Pakistan had substantially expanded the list of items that could be exported by the Indian private sector as a gesture of their earnest desire to expand trade with India. A perusal of the list revealed how fictitious and non-serious it was, including even items like aeroplanes, and it belied what Humayun Khan professed.

In an attempt to give some meaningful content to the two-way trade, I initiated a proposal, taking cognizance of the fact that both India and Pakistan had gone into collaboration with Japan to manufacture the Suzuki car. While we had the usual phased production programme in the collaboration agreement, we were still going to be dependent on imports from Japan for a considerable period of time. Given the trend of the strengthening of the Japanese Yen, our respective companies could face serious financial issues importing from Japan. However, if the two countries were to coordinate their respective phased production programmes, we could complement each other's requirements and thereby reduce dependence on imports from Japan. I am aware that, as a follow-up, an exploratory delegation from Pakistan did visit Maruti but unfortunately, due to the prevailing estranged atmosphere, there was no meaningful outcome.

The Commerce Ministry is the nodal ministry for ESCAP. As the national focal point for ESCAP, I had to visit Bangkok occasionally to attend inter-governmental meetings. The ministerial-level Commission Session was held once a year which was normally attended by the Commerce Minister, with the Commerce Secretary leading the preceding official segment of the Session. Occasionally, Commission Sessions were hosted by member countries and it became almost customary to have every alternate Session away from the headquarters. Several countries came forward to play host, among them being China, Japan (during the 'Sakura' or cherry blossom season), Indonesia, South Korea and India.

Commerce Secretary Prem Kumar, unlike his predecessor, was inclined to devote more time and attention to GATT/WTO than to an organisation like ESCAP, which he did not view as a trade negotiating forum. Hence, work relating to ESCAP was mainly executed at my level as Joint Secretary. India was looked upon by many delegations from developing countries as an effective spokesperson, especially in articulating their interests on issues of common concern and when the need for a united front was imperative to counter opposing positions taken by developed countries. Normally, issues relating to economic and social development being of common concern should not create divisions within the developing countries.

There were, however, occasions when there was a strong division within the group of developing countries, involving some contentious issues. One such contentious issue was that of shared water resources involving Bangladesh and India. The bonhomie that existed in the aftermath of Bangladesh's independence dissipated under successive military rulers after the assassination of Sheikh Mujibur Rahman, as they tried to assert their legitimacy and authority by adopting an anti-

India stance. The sharing of the Ganges river water emerged as one of the crucial political issues in their anti-India campaign. Although the two countries had a bilateral mechanism to discuss and resolve such issues, repeated attempts were made by Bangladesh to raise the issue of shared water resources in various multilateral fora, in particular in the ESCAP annual ministerial sessions since late 1980s. And each time, India had to thwart the attempts by the Bangladesh delegation to mandate the ESCAP secretariat to get involved, asserting the cardinal rule that there had to be consensus among countries concerned on an issue for the secretariat to undertake any work related thereto.

During Kibria's tenure as Executive Secretary (1981-1991), being a former Foreign Secretary of Bangladesh, the Bangladesh delegations felt more emboldened to raise that issue which made our task in resisting more difficult and often resulting in the discussions becoming more acrimonious. I must, however, admit to Executive Secretary Kibria's credit that he personally appeared to maintain a neutral position throughout, knowing what pressures he must have been under from the Bangladesh government. He perhaps left it to his Special Assistant, Enam Chowdhary, also from Bangladesh, who seemed to be conniving with the country's delegation to push this issue in the Commission Sessions. Soon after Chowdhary left ESCAP and returned to the Bangladesh foreign ministry, he reportedly assured his government that he would have the issue of shared water resources included in the work programme of the secretariat at the forthcoming Commission Session.

The Commission Session was hosted by Indonesia and Ali Alatas, Foreign Minister of Indonesia, was the Chairman of the Session. On behalf of the Bangladesh delegation, Enam Chowdhary made a vociferous appeal to get the secretariat to address the issue of shared water resources but failed to achieve a consensus. He tried to make a last ditch effort to interject some enabling language into the report but we resisted it vehemently since it did not accurately reflect the discussions. Faced with an impasse, the Chairman decided to meet the two delegations separately to arrive at a compromise. Our position was unambiguous that the report could not include decisions purported to have been taken but which were inconsistent with the proceedings. I recall Ali Alatas turning to Chowdhary and telling him, 'Don't try to achieve in words what you can't achieve in substance'. A visibly shaken Chowdhary had to retreat, and raising the issue of shared water resources had been laid to rest for good. In 1996, India and Bangladesh signed the Ganges river water bilateral treaty under the more India-friendly leadership of Sheikh Hasina.

At the Commission Session in 1988, Executive Secretary Kibria approached me to check whether I would be interested in taking up an assignment in the ESCAP secretariat as Chief of the International Trade and Tourism Division. Subsequently, Chiefs of Divisions were re-designated as Directors. The post had fallen vacant and he wanted to check with me before making a dèmarche to the Government of India. He said he had been impressed with my performance in ESCAP meetings and he needed an effective leader for the flagship Division. I was excited at the prospect of working at the international level and so expressed my willingness to take on the assignment. Soon thereafter, a formal request was sent to the Government of India through the Indian Embassy in Bangkok. Prem Kumar, Commerce Secretary, forwarded Kibria's request with his recommendation to the Department of Personnel in the Home Ministry for processing my secondment to ESCAP. As information spread, some IAS officers got active to have their name recommended instead. Establishment Officer J.C. Lynn called the Commerce Secretary and informed him that he had been approached by a few officers, including one who was my former colleague in the Commerce Ministry and was already on assignment to ESCAP. He had conveyed to Lynn that as he was senior to me in the IAS, he would face the ignominy of serving under me.

Prem Kumar called me to his office to convey the message to me and in my presence called Lynn and told him that we could not carry IAS seniority to the United Nations. India had no lien to the post offered, so he emphasized that we must send the name of the officer who had the best chance of being selected, especially in the face of attempts by other countries to have their national appointed. He insisted that as far as the Commerce Ministry was concerned, I was the preferred candidate. Lynn still had reservations in approving someone who had been requested for by name, as he felt, it compromised the government's discretion. He, however, ultimately agreed to send my name but only as one of a panel of three names recommended by the government. At the top of the panel was Kutty Nair who, as Deputy Commissioner, had been my senior when I was posted in Hoshiarpur. The second was Bagchi, who was also a Joint Secretary in the Commerce Ministry, but my senior by a few years. My name was at the bottom of the list!

On receipt of the panel of names, Executive Secretary Kibria expressed to me that he was taken aback, as he had specifically asked for my secondment. He, therefore, ignored the panel and proceeded with the processing of my appointment. His recommendation nominating me had to be approved by the Appointment Board at the UN Headquarters in New York. During that time, A.N. Verma had taken over as Commerce Secretary and he had asked Ambassador Prakash Shah, in the Permanent Mission of India to UN, to pursue and support my nomination. However, the Board in its first consideration did not approve my name on the ground of nationality, as India was one of the 'over-represented' countries in the UN system and hence normally not eligible for new appointments. Kibria requested the Board, headed by eminent and respected Under-Secretary-General Nitin Desai to review the decision, when he would personally attend to explain the merits of his recommendation. Kibria must have made a very effective presentation as the Board finally approved my appointment. I remain eternally grateful to him for having given me the opportunity to work at the international level. It was the ideal progression in my career from sub-national to national to international level.

As I had completed my five-year tenure with Central government, I had to return to the Punjab government before my departure for Bangkok, which is the headquarters of ESCAP. I proceeded on leave to prepare and complete all the formalities for the major shift in my career and in our lives. The Punjab government had to find a post for me for a short while before I proceeded to ESCAP. Consequently, I was posted for about a week as Director, Punjab Institute of Public Administration.

There was the usual spate of farewell parties in Delhi, the final and most memorable being the day I was golfed out by my friends, Mukhi, Anil Virmani and Vineet Virmani. We teed off early on a chilly morning in November, which did not matter because we had enough whiskey and beer with us to keep us warm and enjoy the round of golf. That was followed by more alcoholic beverages till early evening at the club. After that I attended a reception for the visiting Russian President Mikhail Gorbachev followed by a get-together with my batch mates over cocktails and finally, a farewell dinner by my old school friend Ini and his wife Hemi. I travelled to Bangkok by myself. Madhu had to wind up her flourishing business as interior designer. Moreover, we were expecting our third child and so I needed to first organize accommodation in Bangkok before she and the children arrived. They followed me a few months later in March.

10

National to International: The United Nations

There is nothing noble in being superior to some other man.
The true nobility is in being superior to your previous self.
—Indian proverb

I joined the United Nations ESCAP in November 1988 as Chief, International Trade and Tourism Division. Executive Secretary Kibria wanted me to join the secretariat before the legislative meeting of the Committee for International Trade, which was to be serviced by the Division. I had arrived just a week before the meeting and in that short time I had to familiarize myself with the documents that had been prepared for the meeting. I knew I would have to take responsibility for the documents in the preparation of which I had no role. Conducting the meeting would not be problematic as I had attended several ESCAP intergovernmental meetings including previous meetings of the Committee on International Trade, albeit as a government delegate. I, therefore, looked upon the forthcoming meeting as a great opportunity to meet delegations from member countries, and equally important for them to get to know me, as Chief of the Division. The meeting went off well and those who had not known me earlier expressed their appreciation that in such a short time, I was able to conduct the meeting and participate in the discussions effectively.

I settled down quickly to revive the Division, which had been without effective leadership for quite a while, to being once again the flagship division of ESCAP. I had the advantage of having seen the work of the secretariat from the perspective of a member government and so was fully sensitized to the task ahead. The main personal adjustment I needed to make was to work in a multi-cultural environment. The professional staff members hailed from different countries and came with their own sensitivities, unlike in India where one had worked in a more homogeneous environment. The converse was equally true, as the staff had to adjust to my style of management which tended to be firmer than the softer approach common in the UN culture. In my first meeting with my staff, I encouraged them, repeating Abid Hussein's 'mantra', to enjoy their work as only then they could give their best. I assured them that I would endeavour to provide a conducive and happy work environment in the Division.

There was soon a difficult issue I had to deal with. A permanent professional staff member hailing from Singapore was not doing any meaningful work and apparently had not been doing so long before I came, but no one wanted to deal with his non-performance as that would involve some strict and perhaps even punitive action. I brought that matter to the attention of the Executive Secretary and was surprised to learn that he was already aware of the problem and had acquiesced in the matter. He informed me that to take any punitive action like dismissal, it was necessary to prepare a full record for at least two years before the case could be submitted to the headquarters for appropriate action. The particular staff member's past annual performance reports had not only glossed over his non-performance but had, in fact, shown him to have achieved considerable work, and these reports had been signed and countersigned at various levels in routine, including finally by the Executive Secretary himself. That meant that a fresh record had to be created.

It shocked me that such malaise could exist in the UN system and a person could survive without doing an iota of work. So, I was determined to take that case to its logical conclusion. However, I felt that it would be only fair that the staff member should be given a final opportunity, so I called him and tried to mentor him, clearly stating my observation that he had neither put a pen to paper nor spoken a word in any Division meeting. As one last chance, I gave him some specific work to complete within a given timeframe. As expected, he failed to even make an attempt to do so.

When the time came for his annual performance evaluation, his own statement of considerable work done by him had been endorsed by his immediate supervisor, the Section Chief, and forwarded to me for my endorsement. I called the Section Chief and asked him if he had seen any of the work purported to have been done. He sheepishly admitted he had not and neither could he explain on what basis he had endorsed the statement, except to imply that it was out of compassion for a colleague. I told him that he had the option to either revise his report or I would record on his own report that he was not fit to be a supervisor. He revised his report and after two annual performance evaluation reports, we were ready to submit the case for termination of service due to non-performance. It took unduly long within the secretariat to process the case and even longer at the UN Headquarters, illustrating how rare it was for anyone in the UN system to seek punitive action against a recalcitrant staff member. This case definitely blew the myth that to dismiss a permanent staff member in the UN system was well-nigh impossible. It also established very early in my career in the UN my reputation of being a no-nonsense supervisor.

During senior staff meetings, which the Executive Secretary would hold weekly, I found that unlike my peers, I could relate our discussions to ground realities, whereas most others had only academic knowledge. The advantage of having been in the IAS was the actual experience one had gained in diverse areas. While my own direct responsibility was related to trade, foreign investment and tourism, I could participate meaningfully in discussions relating to poverty alleviation, industrial development, social development, etc. Moreover, having attended five annual Commission Sessions as a government delegate, servicing my first Commission Session as a member of the secretariat was certainly different but not difficult.

On 14 July 1989, when the world celebrated Bastille Day, we celebrated the birth of our third daughter, Raisa. This time too it had to be Dr Soonawala, who flew in especially from Mumbai to do the caesarean procedure. His reputation as a specialist with his own method of doing caesareans had already reached Bangkok and so it was not too difficult in getting the hospital to allow him to handle the case, of course with a local gynaecologist to assist him, since he was not licensed to practice in Thailand. In fact, the local doctors welcomed the opportunity to observe Dr Soonawala's procedure.

Our two elder daughters, Ravina and Aushima, were attending school at the highly reputed, International School of Bangkok (ISB). As we found out later, it is really an American school for international children, as the faculty seemed to view a student's demeanour, accent and even style of dressing through an American prism. One day we received a note from the School Counsellor requesting a meeting with us. Madhu and I went to her office wondering what could have prompted the request for such a meeting. The Counsellor, as expected an American lady, said there was a problem relating to Aushima. She felt that perhaps, having a newborn baby at home, we were inadvertently ignoring Aushima and so she was developing complexes, and as a result, she was lying to gain popularity among her classmates.

We were shocked to hear that as Aushima was always an outgoing and happy child, so we asked the Counsellor to elaborate. She said that when the children in her class were asked to talk about their families, Aushima had said that her grandmother was a princess from a royal family. In complete shock and disgust, I asked the Counsellor how much she knew about India and the fact that there were many princely states there. It was obvious that the Counsellor was totally ignorant about India and was viewing the background of international children from an American point of view. She had obviously erred seriously in presuming that Aushima was lying and thereby subjecting her to trauma. In disdain, I told the Counsellor that it was she who needed counselling and we were not going to accept her misconceived behaviour.

We withdrew our children from ISB and decided to send them to an international school for girls that had just opened in Mussoorie, India. The children spent a year in boarding there but then we felt that they were really missing out seeing Raisa grow. We brought them back to Bangkok and got them admitted in the Ruamrudee International School, which seemed to be much more suitable for our children. The children were much happier there because of the school's more conducive environment that they had been accustomed to. A few years later, the school shifted to its own campus some distance away from the city meaning much longer travel time in school buses, but Ravina and Aushima took it easily in their stride and completed their graduation from there.

Also a matter of great concern to us, especially during the initial years in Bangkok, was that our children should not lose contact with our families in India, especially the children of my two brothers. Their bonding during childhood was extremely important; otherwise they could grow up as strangers to their cousins. Madhu was pivotal in encouraging Nano and Minoo, our sisters-in-law, to send their children to Bangkok, whenever they had school holidays.

Rajive and Minoo's daughter, Ritika, the leader of the generation pack, visited us in Chandigarh and later in Bangkok. She got into art very early and gifted us with her very first painting, which till today adorns our writing table. Their son, Rishal, spent a good six months with us doing an internship with UNDP. Ricky and Nano's two daughters visited us more frequently. Shikha stayed with us almost a year when she and Ravina did a course in gemmology. Later she and Ravina went together to a university in Seattle. Shivangini also spent considerable time with us, as a child and then distinguished herself, by doing an assignment with the International Labour Organisation in Bangkok. Hence, while our children grew up away from India, they grew up bonding very closely with their cousins, and happily even today they remain a very close-knit family.

Back to my work. In a short time, my Division had become much more active with larger financial support from donor countries for technical assistance projects. In fact, it became the largest recipient of extra-budgetary financial support and, in reality, became the flagship Division in the secretariat. Our technical assistance projects related to analysis-based advocacy of trade policy issues and options in the context of trade negotiations under GATT/WTO, as well as capacity building in the areas of trade promotion and trade facilitation including development of trade information services. As our technical assistance activities increased so did my travel in the region, as many of the activities were held in different countries, often depending on the donor country's preference.

As I was settling down in my work in the secretariat, a group of UN staff members from different agencies came to meet me to request my assistance in their plans to set up a UN school in Bangkok. My immediate reaction was that, having only recently arrived in the UN, I might not be able to devote time to their venture. But the idea of establishing a truly international UN school was certainly appealing, especially after the experience with ISB. They assured me that I would not be required to devote too much time, as they primarily needed someone at a senior level to help out if and when required. I consented to join them and chaired the group.

Our first task was to get a feasibility study done for which we required funds. I spoke to Executive Secretary Kibria and he agreed to have a meeting with heads of all UN agencies in Bangkok to solicit their involvement. At the meeting, there was general endorsement of the project and some agencies backed it with financial contribution, the largest amount coming from ESCAP. An inter-agency Working Group for International Education was set up and I was appointed its chairman. With the corpus of funds in hand, we set out to get a feasibility study done for which we selected Joseph Blaney, a former Director of the United Nations International School in New York, who had the requisite experience. Thereafter, we approached the UN Secretary-General Boutros Boutros-Ghali for approval of establishing a UN school but, unfortunately, he declined approval as the UN was then facing serious financial crisis due to the Americans holding back their annual contribution.

However, by then the expatriate community in Bangkok had also got energized to support the establishment of a truly international school. We applied for a licence. The then interim government of professionals, headed by Anand Panyarachun, relaxed the existing ban on new international schools and granted us the licence, keeping in view that the proposal had some linkage with the UN. We decided to name the school New International School of Thailand (NIST) as it was the most neutral name we could agree on in the short time available to us. We registered a Foundation for International Education, as the legal entity, and I was its first Chairman. We started looking for new premises and visited various sites, including some established Thai schools, which were keen to convert to an international school, but none were suitable for our purpose. There was then a newspaper advertisement by the Church of Christ, Bangkok, to rent out their property, which had been vacated by the International School of Bangkok (ISB), having moved to their own campus.

While we were still mulling over the feasibility of our renting the prime property in the heart of the city, the University of Maryland approached us with an offer to join them in co-renting the property. Their plan was to run an evening campus, whereas we were interested in a day school, so it looked to be an ideal partnership. We jointly negotiated with the Church of Christ and signed the lease deed. Then the most unexpected happened when the University of Maryland was refused a licence by the Thai government and they withdrew from the lease agreement. We were suddenly faced with the utmost untenable situation of not being ready to start a school and the rent clock already ticking! Emergency measures had to be taken. We took a working capital loan from the Siam Commercial Bank, which is the UN bank, against personal guarantees furnished by some of us. To get some inflow of funds, we immediately hired a few teachers and started tuition classes for English language and simultaneously initiated action on admissions for the oncoming school year, which was just a few months away. In August 1992, we were prepared to start with primary school classes, having done emergency recruitment of a Headmaster, teaching faculty and support staff.

Ravina and Aushima continued their studies in their Ruamrudee School, as they were already in middle school. Raisa graduated from NIST and currently my granddaughter, Riana, is studying there. I can say with pride and confidence that NIST is a truly international school with UN values enshrined in its constitution. Now in its 30th year, it is the premier educational institution in Thailand with over 1600 children from more than 56 countries. I continue to be associated with the school as a Founding Member on the Foundation.

Reflecting on my career, I have had a significant involvement with educational institutions. Beginning with my alma mater, where as a member of the school board I was deeply involved in restructuring the governing body, later as Administrator of a rural college in Punjab and more recently in the establishment of an international school. After so many years of a happy and eventful life in Bangkok, I feel a great sense of satisfaction having made a permanent contribution to the architecture of international educational institutions in Thailand.

In the early 1990s, there were significant changes within the ESCAP secretariat. Kibria had retired and he was succeeded by Rafeeuddin Ahmed as Executive Secretary. Originally from Pakistan, he had a long and distinguished career in the UN system. Unlike Kibria, who tended to be slightly formal and appeared distant from staff members, Rafi, as he liked to be called, was completely informal and mixed freely with staff members regardless of their rank. This was also a time when there was a paradigm shift in ESCAP's work programme. ESCAP member countries, in response to the ongoing intensification of the forces of globalization, resolved in a Commission Session to restructure its subsidiary structure and following that, the secretariat's work programme was also restructured from sectoral to thematic. The major thematic sub-programme was 'regional economic cooperation', which included the secretariat's work related to international trade and tourism, foreign investment, industry and technology transfer, and transport and communications. This corresponded to the changed legislative structure, with the Committee for Regional Economic Cooperation and its Steering Group replacing the three sectoral Committees. The Steering Group was intended to be a forum for experts to deliberate on issues and submit their report to policymakers in the Committee.

I was appointed as Chairman of the Working Group on Regional Economic Cooperation to coordinate the thematic work programme and, as such, it was my responsibility to ensure that the work of the related Divisions was cohesive and consistent with the theme, especially in their submissions to the Steering Group and the Committee on Regional Economic Cooperation. The transition into thematic programming was a challenging process, as changes requiring a changed mindset tend to be resisted. The Directors of the other two Divisions were resentful to having their work being overseen by a peer. My approach had to be and was principle-based, and so I could deal with them effectively whenever there was a dissenting note. The problem would often occur when the secretariat's reports of the proceedings in the legislative meetings of the Steering Group and the Committee were submitted to the Commission Sessions, which would include mandates given by member countries to the secretariat to undertake certain activities as constituents of the work programme on regional economic cooperation.

There was a tendency among some Division Directors to interpolate into the secretariat's report of the proceedings, mandates that they sought but were never given. Hence, while vetting and giving my approval of the secretariat's report, I would strike out all such inaccurate interpolations in the interest of maintaining integrity, which annoyed my peers. One Director, with tacit support of the other, even went to the extent of submitting a representation to the Executive Secretary, accusing me of being autocratic. My response was simple that I could not have double standards, one for my Division and another for the others. They soon learnt to accept my style of functioning, albeit with an undercurrent of resentment.

It became almost customary that meetings of the Steering Group were held away from the secretariat, as several member countries were interested in hosting them. Among them were India, which hosted the first meeting in Delhi, and Japan, which offered to host a meeting at Chitose in the northern Hokkaido Island. A new airport had been built in Chitose which would shorten travelling time on the northern routes, so the Japanese government was keen to give the airport exposure through an international event. During my preparatory visit to Chitose, there was discernible enthusiasm among the local authorities, especially as it was the first international event they were going to host. At the time of the meeting, the whole city was dressed up with welcome banners and posters, giving unprecedented publicity to the event. The Japanese, in the true style of their generous hospitality, included in the programme a trip after the meeting to Sapporo for the participants to witness the winter ice festival. The hosts provided warm clothing to all participants, having got information on their sizes in advance of the meeting.

During the preparatory visit to Chitose, I was taken to the Salmon Aquarium, a museum where one can learn everything about salmon and view them in the Chitose River. The salmon leave the river as fishling for the sea and return to the river when they are ready to spawn. They then swim upstream and are caught in what is called Indian wheel. The Indian wheel is similar to what one sees in Indian villages, driven by cattle or camels, going around in a circle and water is pumped out in buckets. In Chitose, it's not water but salmon coming out of the buckets.

Chitose was celebrating the centenary of the Indian wheel and had brought out 'sake' bottles with the Indian wheel on the label to commemorate the event. During a dinner hosted by the Mayor of Chitose, I was amazed to learn that after the salmon is caught, it is bisected and the roe sack is taken out to make caviar and the salmon is processed to produce fish meal for poultry. The salmon, after having swum upstream and undergone the extraction of its eggs, is no longer fit for the finicky Japanese pallet. I remarked that it appeared to be such a waste of protein-rich food which could be processed and exported to needy countries or even supplied to refugee camps. Moreover, fish meal could be an item Japan could provide a market for import from developing countries. The Mayor responded that they had never thought on those lines and agreed to my suggestion to meet with a team of experts to examine the feasibility of any alternate use of the salmon. Subsequently, I asked an organisation, INFOFISH, based in Malaysia, to send a team to Chitose, which it did but, as we later realised, it is not easy to dismantle something as traditional as that, even in Japan.

China was another country which was a very active member of ESCAP and notwithstanding its status as a developing country, it was an important donor of extra-budgetary resources for the secretariat to undertake technical assistance projects. Funding was, however, provided selectively for projects which were consistent with China's own priorities and the project activities such as seminars and training courses had to be held within China. I viewed it as a clever use of its funds, as ostensibly China was a donor country but it leveraged the opportunity to include a large number of Chinese participants in the training activities conducted by international experts. After the Tiananmen Square incident in 1989, there was an understandable lull in organizing project activities in China, as international reaction was generally very negative. However, after a lapse of a few months, I organized an inter-governmental meeting in Beijing, which, in a sense, was breaking the ice after the Tiananmen incident.

The Chinese government, realizing the significance of this meeting, went out of its way to extend host facilities and made the unprecedented gesture of inviting the participants to the Great Hall of the People to meet with Prime Minister Li Peng. The format of the meeting was similar to when the Premier met world leaders, that is, I was sitting next to him and an interpreter behind us. The Premier was extremely pleased to see the international gathering and grateful to ESCAP for having organized the event in Beijing. This gesture on our part kept us in good books with the Chinese government for future support and cooperation.

As Chairman of the ESCAP Appointments and Promotion Board, I had to deal with an unprecedented difficult situation when I did not endorse Executive Secretary Rafeeuddin Ahmed's recommendation for promotion of a staff member in a particular case. The Division Director concerned approached me before the Board meeting to ensure his recommendation, which had been endorsed by the Executive Secretary, was approved. I remained non-committal but realised that it could be an acid test of my objective and impartial style of functioning. The Board, consisting of senior staff members, reviewed and decided all cases at the professional level for appointment or promotion in the secretariat after the Executive Secretary had made his recommendation. While considering a case, the Board had to, inter alia, ensure that there were no collaterals who might have merited but were denied due consideration in the process. In that particular case of promotion, the staff member recommended by the Executive Secretary was a very high-profile individual.

In the process of checking on collaterals, I found that there was another staff member in the same Division who appeared to have an equally good track record and had been at the existing level longer than the recommended candidate. As there was no cogent explanation forthcoming why she was overlooked, I insisted that she must be given priority consideration and the Board agreed with me to supersede the Executive Secretary's recommendation and promote the other staff member. I had neither ever met nor even previously heard the name of the newly promoted staff member. It was a principled decision, based strictly on an established objective criterion. Since that was perhaps one solitary case where the Executive Secretary's recommendation had been superseded, I did later talk to Rafi and he appeared at least outwardly very understanding. Quite clearly, the Division Director concerned had not brought the matter of overlooking the collateral to the attention of the Executive Secretary. It did, however, create ripples in the secretariat and some tension with the Director of the Division concerned. I must, however, add that the staff member whom we had not promoted was also very competent and deserving and was promoted in due course. In time, with her better understanding of my being objective, we became very cordial and mutually respecting colleagues. Very importantly, this incident did not in any way create any strain in my standing with the Executive Secretary.

When I had completed five years on secondment with ESCAP, the Indian government promptly asked the Executive Secretary to release me for return to India. Rafi was very keen that I should continue in view of my additional responsibilities and involvement in the process of the secretariat's transition to thematic programming. After consulting me to confirm my willingness to continue, he wrote back to the Government of India, through the Indian Embassy in Bangkok, the following letter:

> As you know, ESCAP is undergoing a transition into thematic programming following the restructuring of its subsidiary structure, as decided by the Commission at its 48th session in April 1992. The implementation of the new programme structure will begin in January 1994. As a valuable member of the staff at the senior decision-making level, Mr. Sawhney has been playing a very important role in the process of transition as well as in the evolving new programme structure. In addition to his duties as Chief

of the International Trade and Tourism Division, Mr. Sawhney is also Chairman of the Working Group on the sub-programme on Regional Economic Cooperation in the secretariat, in which capacity he serves as one of the three main focal points for coordination and follow-up of the thematic sub-programmes adopted by the Commission. He is also the main substantive Division Chief responsible for servicing of the newly established Committee for Regional Economic Cooperation as well as its Steering Group. In fact, following the Commission's decision to give focused attention to strengthening of regional economic cooperation, the Steering Group had taken a major initiative and adopted the action programme for regional economic cooperation in trade and investment. This was provided further impetus when the Commission, at its last session in April 1993, adopted resolution 49/1 on the implementation of the action programme for regional economic cooperation in trade and investment, effecting detailed guidance on the matter and requesting me to report to it annually on the progress and implementation of the action programme. It is pertinent to recall here that the foundation of this important initiative was laid in New Delhi when the Government of India generously hosted the First Meeting of the Steering Group of the Committee for Regional Economic Cooperation in November 1992. This important transition period also coincided with an important programme on "Strengthening capacity for growth, trade and investment" initiated by UNDP during ICP V, under which ESCAP would remain responsible for implementation of a major multi-year UNDP funded project on "Exploitation of business opportunities", which is indicative of the intensive nature of activities characterizing the significant transition that ESCAP's trade and investment programme is currently undergoing, in which Mr. Sawhney plays a key leading role.

Taking the above circumstances into account, I consider continuation of Mr. Sawhney's services with the secretariat at this time to be vital for the future of ESCAP. Mr. Sawhney has indicated his willingness to continue his employment with the secretariat. However, he hopes very much that extension of his appointment would continue on the basis of secondment from the government service.

It would be pertinent to keep in view that the forthcoming 50th session of the Commission, which will be generously hosted by the Government of India in April 1994, will surely give further important directions to the secretariat for following up on the various initiatives taken by the Commission in recent years. Furthermore, in the light of the various resolutions and decisions of the General Assembly and the relevant rules and regulations of the United Nations, it remains quite uncertain if the Headquarters will ever agree to waive existing restrictions to favourably consider appointment of an Indian national to a senior position in the secretariat, in the event of Mr. Sawhney's departure.

Under these circumstances, I would be grateful if you could kindly convey my request to the Government of India to consider granting special dispensation in order to enable Mr. Sawhney to continue his services with the secretariat on secondment from the Government.

The Executive Secretary's letter was forthright in conveying two important messages. First, that I was playing a very important role in the transition process in the secretariat and hence continuation of my services at that time was 'vital for the future of ESCAP'. Second, in the event of my departure, it was very unlikely that an Indian national could replace me. In response to the Executive Secretary's request, the Government of India agreed to a two-year extension in my secondment to ESCAP with an ultimatum that it would not agree to any further extension. The then Indian Ambassador Ranjit Gupta accordingly communicated to the Executive Secretary Government's approval together with the ultimatum.

I felt slighted by the tone and content of the communication and conveyed my feelings to Ranjit with whom I had a personal rapport. I felt that the government could have exercised more discretion and have conveyed the ultimatum separately to me, with equal or even more effect, instead of letting it be put in the public domain and thereby compromising my position in the secretariat. I felt that as far as the secretariat was concerned, I should have been seen to have the unconditional support of my government and not as one faced with an ultimatum on his future tenure.

It is indeed unfortunate that a seasoned bureaucracy as in India can be insensitive and devoid of finesse in dealing with matters having international ramifications. Did they not realise that other member countries would immediately get active to have their national occupying that post, considering its importance? In contrast, countries like Bangladesh dealt with such matters with much greater sensitivity and discretion, as I had witnessed, having had one of its senior foreign service officers working in my Division for several years and facing a similar situation. Quite inexplicably, our government chose to ignore that I was the only Indian holding a senior substantive position in ESCAP and its significance in a situation where getting Indian nationals in senior positions in the UN system was extremely difficult, if not impossible.

The question, whether it was really prudent to enforce a domestic policy regardless of the consequences, begs an answer. In fact, I had earlier suggested to the Foreign Ministry that in such a situation where induction of Indians into the UN system was extremely difficult, the government should identify the UN agencies and the posts therein, which might be of priority interest and try and get Indians, already in the system, to those positions, so we could achieve. at least quality if not quantity, in our presence in the UN system. Unfortunately, issues such as this get too personalised and hence the larger interest of the country is lost to narrow-minded considerations.

I happened to be in Delhi at the time of Rajiv Gandhi's assassination in May 1991. I felt a sense of personal loss as we had been acquainted since our college days. Even as Prime Minister, he continued to acknowledge my presence whenever he saw me sitting in the officers' gallery in the Lok Sabha, by mouthing 'how are you?' with a smile and slight nod of the head. Every year we received season's greetings signed by him and Sonia. His assassination, therefore, felt as a deeply saddening personal loss. I made it a point to be there when Rajiv's body lay in state and assisted in escorting foreign leaders who had arrived to pay their last respects.

The Congress was in disarray having lost their charismatic leader and that too at such a crucial time when campaigning for the general elections was in its final stages. I accompanied my father-in-law Romesh Bhandari to Narasimha Rao's house when he went to urge him to come out of retirement to lead the party. He had been Foreign Secretary when Narasimha Rao was the Foreign Minister and so enjoyed the rapport to speak to him in confidence. We met over tea and I noticed the slight trembling in Narasimha Rao's hands, as he drank tea. I later remarked to my father-in-law that Narasimha Rao looked physically very frail to take on such a huge responsibility, but he was confident that if there was any one, it was he who could bail the Congress out of the disastrous situation. Well, Narasimha Rao did become the Prime Minister. I met him again when he visited Bangkok on a bilateral official visit and he certainly looked far more robust and alert.

On his visit to Bangkok, PM Narasimha Rao was accompanied by A.N. Verma, Principal Secretary, Montek Ahluwalia, Chief Economic Advisor, and Ganesan, Commerce Secretary. Ambassador A.N. Ram requested Executive Secretary Rafeeuddin Ahmed and me to meet the Prime Minister in his hotel room one afternoon to give him an overview on the Asia-Pacific regional situation. At the meeting, Narasimha Rao first turned to Rafi and assured him that although the government might not openly acknowledge, it did take into account ESCAP policy prescriptions when considering various policy options, as the UN had the great advantage of being a neutral organisation.

The Prime Minister then turned to me and asked why China was able to attract high technology investment whereas India had not been able to. I explained that China had started its reform and liberalization process in the mid-1970s and so had a head start over India. I pointed out that in China, international trade and foreign investment was a national effort, as every provincial government actively participated and was empowered to take decisions on foreign investments, albeit within certain parameters, whereas in India, the state governments had no meaningful role in promoting Indian exports or attracting foreign investment.

Having worked in Punjab, I gave the example of the Punjab Export Corporation which was considered by the state government a convenient organisation to park an unwanted police officer to head it. Having worked in promoting industrial development while in Punjab, and now viewing it externally, I visualized that any potential foreign investor, having to deal only with the Central government, would take a macro look at India as a mosaic of opportunity and problems and could therefore feel discouraged by any untoward happening, natural or man-made, in any part of the country. However, if an interested foreign investor was to directly approach an empowered state government, he would have more confidence, knowing that he would be dealing with that government in future as well and would not be deterred by any untoward happening in another part of India.

I summed it up by saying that it was ironical there was more decentralization in decision-making in an undemocratic country like China than in a democracy like India where decision-making was still highly centralized in the Central government. After the Prime Minister returned to India, I received a telephone call from Principal Secretary A.N. Verma, who was also my former boss in the Commerce Ministry, informing me that the Prime Minister had directed a task force to look into the issues that I had raised and so I should consider my meeting with the Prime Minister to have been very meaningful.

As part of the regional economic cooperation thematic sub-programme, I proposed the institutionalization of dialogue between ESCAP and the subregional organisations, viz., Association of Southeast Asian Nations (ASEAN), Economic Cooperation

Organization (ECO), Pacific Forum and South Asian Association for Regional Cooperation (SAARC), both individually and collectively. We created a forum for regular meetings with the executive heads of subregional organisations to explore and strengthen intra- and inter-subregional cooperation, with ESCAP, as a regional organisation, acting as a facilitator and a bridge between the subregional organisations. Specific areas were identified where the subregional organisations could learn from each other's experiences.

A major area of interest was the establishment of a free trade area at the subregional level in which the ASEAN had made some headway with ASEAN Free Trade Area (AFTA) and SAARC was pursuing a similar SAFTA (South Asian Free Trade Area). A constraining factor was that while ASEAN and SAARC had some complementarity, ECO and the Pacific Forum were geographically remote and so the scope for their cooperation with the other subregional organisations was limited. Hence, for ECO and the Pacific Forum the emphasis was more on their cooperation with ESCAP. Even on cooperation between ASEAN and SAARC, the former was reticent to have institutionalized cooperation, as it feared it might be confronted with the fallout of the tense and acrimonious India-Pakistan relations.

There was a significant change with expansion in ESCAP's constituency when the Soviet Union, following Gorbachev's perestroika and glasnost policies, disintegrated into independent countries. The Soviet Union was a 'non-regional member' of ESCAP like the USA, the UK, France and the Netherlands, as former colonial powers in this region. The Central Asian Republics—Kazakhstan, Kyrgyzstan, Tajikistan, Turkmenistan and Uzbekistan—on becoming independent countries, asserted their Asian identity and thus became members of ESCAP. In addition, other former Soviet Republics like

Azerbaijan, Georgia and Armenia also became members of ESCAP. They also continued to be treated as members of the United Nations Economic Commission for Europe (UNECE) as successor states of the Soviet Union, which was its regional member. In due course, President Nursultan Nazarbayev of Kazakhstan requested UN Secretary-General Kofi Annan to establish a separate UN regional commission for the five Central Asian countries. As that was not considered feasible, given the financial constraints the UN was facing, the Secretary-General directed the two regional commissions, ESCAP and UNECE, of which these countries were members, to jointly formulate a special programme for their economic and social development. On behalf of ESCAP, the Executive Secretary appointed me as Coordinator, in addition to my other responsibilities, for developing and implementing what became known as the Special Programme for the Economies of Central Asia (SPECA). Coincidentally, the acronym SPECA has the same alphabets as ESCAP!

SPECA had two dimensions, internal and external. The internal dimension was to assist the former command economies in their transition to market economies and to foster intra-Central Asian cooperation among independent countries. The external dimension was to develop and strengthen their integration with the Asian and European regions. To develop the programme in both its dimensions, joint visits of the two Executive Secretaries, supported by the two Coordinators, were planned to meet the President of each country in order to understand his aspirations and priorities for his country. We soon realised that the process of intra-cooperation was going to be very challenging, especially as we were dealing with countries that were now fiercely exerting their status as independent entities after years of being vassal states to Moscow and so much depended on the personality of the President and his equation with his counterparts in other countries. The Presidents of all the Central Asian countries were former General/First Secretaries in the Communist Party, the only exception being Kyrgyzstan, which had a former Professor as President. Kyrgyzstan and Tajikistan had two water towers and the others were dependent on them for water. In turn, Kyrgyzstan and Tajikistan were dependent on the others for their energy requirements. This complementarity could be assumed to be a strong basis for cooperation but it also turned out to be a potential cause of conflict.

Our first visit was to Kazakhstan to meet President Nazarbayev, as he had been instrumental in the UN taking this initiative. His response was understandably positive and he emphatically suggested to accord priority attention to the development of trade and investment as well as transport and communications in the programme. However, our meeting with President Islam Karimov of Uzbekistan was bereft of the enthusiasm that we had witnessed earlier. It was apparent that Karimov was not enthused by the leadership role that Nazarbayev was playing, especially when he himself had entertained aspirations of being the leader. Perhaps, their current relations were predicated on some past history between the two. Karimov focused more on the problem Uzbekistan faced in getting adequate and assured supply of water from Kyrgyzstan for irrigation and less on giving any meaningful input to SPECA. In retaliation to blocking supply of water by Kyrgyzstan, Uzbekistan would reduce oil and gas supply to Kyrgyzstan, especially when their demand was critical during the winter months. We could sense that Uzbekistan's participation in the programme would be low key and so it was.

Turkmenistan was another difficult proposition, as we realised in our first meeting with President Saparmurat Niyazov in Ashgabat. Niyazov was an authoritarian and had established a personality cult of himself with his statues in every street corner, including a revolving gold statue that always faced the sun, as well as a museum dedicated to himself in his lifetime. He wanted the UN to provide his country diversified pipeline routes for the export of hydrocarbons to Europe through Iran, knowing that relations between Europe and Iran were tension-ridden and were also being influenced by the USA's threats of sanctions against Iran. He professed to be following a policy of neutrality but quite inexplicably was reluctant to foster economic cooperation with other Central Asian countries.

The visits to Kyrgyzstan and Tajikistan had to be undertaken by me alone from ESCAP as Executive Secretary Adrianus Mooy was not available then. President Askar Akayev of Kyrgyzstan invited us to Bishkek towards December-end. Mooy was due to go on his Christmas vacation but we decided to go ahead with the visit without him, as it was very difficult to get appointments. Kyrgyzstan is basically an agricultural economy and dependent on Uzbekistan for supply of natural gas. President Akayev was a different kind of personality, having been a former professor, and he enthusiastically discussed his plans for diversification of the economy. My suggestion to provide assistance in developing entrepreneurship for small and medium enterprises was accepted by him with great enthusiasm. He also wanted the programme to include cooperation in the rational and effective use of energy and water resources and sought UN assistance in working out a transboundary water sharing agreement with Kazakhstan relating to the Chu and Talas rivers, flowing from Kyrgyzstan to Kazakhstan. A few years later, an intergovernmental transboundary water commission was established which, inter alia, included the sharing of responsibilities for investment and maintenance of infrastructure like dams and reservoirs for water supply to both countries. It is, however, unfortunate that out of all the Central Asian leaders, Akayev was the first to be ousted for alleged corruption by his family.

The visit to Bishkek, Kyrgyzstan, was also memorable for an entirely different reason. It took me nine days from the day I left and returned to Bangkok for a two-hour meeting with President Akayev, and that too, after having travelled every day. It is indicative of how difficult commuting was to and within Central Asia in those days and especially in winter months when many airports are snowed in and are temporarily shut down. On the first day, I travelled from Bangkok to Delhi; second day, from Delhi to Tashkent but as the airport was snowed in, the flight was diverted to Nukus for about three hours before arriving in Tashkent late evening on the third day. Then from Tashkent to Almaty, but again the flight was diverted to Shymkent and halted for about four hours till Almaty airport was clear; it was the fourth day. Very early next morning we drove from Almaty to Bishkek; it was the fifth day. The meeting with President was on the sixth day. The return on the seventh day was by road to Almaty, a three-hour journey that took eight hours because of heavy snowfall the previous night. On the eighth day, we took a flight to Tashkent; then on to Delhi and departure for Bangkok same night but the flight was cancelled due to fog. It was day nine when I got back to Bangkok! For the UNECE team from Geneva, it was much easier as there was a direct flight to Almaty from where it is about three hours mountainous drive to Bishkek.

The fifth Central Asian country, Tajikistan, was in the midst of a civil war and the UN had declared a level of security threat phase which prohibited UN international staff to travel there. President Emomali Rahmon was, however, insistent that Tajikistan should not be left out of the SPECA-related consultation process. His Ambassador to the UN in New York met the Secretary-General and conveyed President

Rahmon's request, backed with the assurance that the UN delegation would be given full protection and housed in the President's estate. On receiving the Secretary-General's clearance, we planned our joint visit to Dushanbe. Mooy was again unable to go, so it was the Executive Secretary accompanied by the Coordinator from UNECE and I alone from ESCAP. We met President Rahmon and he accorded priority to holding an international economic conference for developing a regional development strategy and attracting foreign investment, with special focus on Tajikistan.

The travel to Tajikistan was yet another memorable experience. The UNECE team had a direct flight to Dushanbe. I had to travel to Delhi and from there to Tashkent from where a heavily guarded motorcade took me to the nearest airport, Khujand in Tajikistan. It was in Khujand two UN personnel had been abducted earlier and hence it was considered a high security risk area warranting extra security arrangements. On arrival in Dushanbe, I was driven straight to the President's Guest House. The sound of firing could be heard en route and throughout the night. Tajikistan being the northern neighbour of Afghanistan gave it strategic importance. Russia continued to maintain a base there which at that time was involved in providing relief to the earthquake-hit Afghanistan. From our perspective, the meeting with President Rahmon was more an exercise that needed to be completed, given the uncertainty over the political situation.

The return journey for me was through the same route through Khujand. As I was transported from Tashkent to Khujand airport under high security, I expected to be received on return with the same security and transport arrangements. We arrived in Khujand in the midst of a severe snowstorm. I waited in the plane, expecting my security escorts to arrive but no one came. I disembarked right into the snowstorm and had to trudge to the terminal building. To my shock, there was no security or the transport there. I was drenched and, having been denied access to the VIP lounge, had to wait in the dilapidated terminal building. Local taxi ('machine') drivers kept approaching me speaking in a language I did not understand and had to physically shun all their attempts to pick up my bag to get me to hire a taxi. Having been a guest of the President, I was not carrying any local currency so buying a cup of coffee was out of the question. There I sat, isolated, from where two abductions had already taken place, feeling cold and vulnerable and fearing I could be the third case of abduction. After more than two hours, the motorcade and security arrived. I was relieved to see them but could not resist expressing my anger and disappointment over their failure to receive me at the airport as promised. The explanation offered was that there had been a miscommunication regarding the time of arrival of the flight from Dushanbe, which was difficult for me to accept.

Despite all the trials and tribulations, SPECA was formally launched in March 1998 with the issuance of the Tashkent Declaration, signed by the Presidents of the five participating countries and the Executive Secretaries of ESCAP and ECE. The Tashkent Declaration acknowledged the communality of economic development interests of the Central Asian countries, emphasized further strengthening of economic ties among them and their economic integration with Asia and Europe. The inaugural function was held in Tashkent intentionally to appease President Karimov and give him the centre stage in the midst of all the Presidents of member states. The grandeur of the function organized by Uzbekistan government appeared to signal that President Karimov was finally enthused by the initiative. Unfortunately, that was not so, as Uzbekistan remained ambivalent in its participation. Its reticence, along with that of Turkmenistan, posed a challenge that we were determined to take on to enlist their active participation. Subsequently, effort was also directed at fostering cooperation between SPECA and other initiatives being taken by international organisations like the Asian Development Bank's initiative—Central Asian Regional Economic Cooperation Programme (CAREC). When the Shanghai Cooperation Organisation (SCO) was created in 2001, in which all the countries, except Turkmenistan, were also members, we made efforts in the initial stage to create synergy between the two initiatives but the lack of positive response from SCO, with its larger membership, indicated that the scope for cooperation was limited.

Another country, which was earlier a satellite country of the Soviet Union, that merited special attention of the UN system, was Mongolia. Mongolia had introduced the multi-party system for the first time and based thereon, parliamentary elections were held successfully. In order to ensure that the new political system would succeed, the United Nations Development Programme (UNDP) organized a conference in Ulaanbaatar, the capital of Mongolia, which was attended by various UN agencies, including ESCAP represented by me, the World Bank, International Monetary Fund, Asian Development Bank and donor countries from Asia and Europe. At the conference, areas were identified and earmarked for assistance from the UN agencies as well as from donor countries in both the economic and social sectors. At the conference, I outlined the significant work ESCAP had previously done in sustainable development and trade in the mineral sector, and based there on, this sector, which is of vital importance to Mongolia's economic development, was assigned to us.

As an expression of their gratitude, the Mongolian government organized a day's trip by a chartered flight to Gobi Desert after the conference. There being no regular airport, we landed on a makeshift strip outlined by white stone markers. Nearby was a small hamlet of dilapidated buildings. On arrival, there were two rather dilapidated buses to transport us across the desert to a museum where dinosaur fossils were kept. We had to be back to the aircraft before dark as without lights on the airstrip, it would not be possible to take off in the dark. As it happened, the bus that I was in, broke down midway and there was no contingency arrangement except for the other bus to do double duty. Consequently, by the time we were back to the airstrip, it was already dark and the pilot was not willing to risk taking off in the dark. We were informed that we would have to stay there till daybreak and were escorted to one of the dilapidated buildings. There were no arrangements for food or even water and neither were these available in the deserted hamlet. Being late October, the temperature started dropping rapidly and the dilapidated building offered little shelter from the chilly winds. Our Mongolian hosts suddenly produced a few bottles of Mongolian vodka on which we had to depend to survive that night. At the first light of day, we were hustled into the aircraft, reeling under the effect of copious gulps of neat Vodka. Some of us were to catch the MIAT flight that morning for Beijing. As there was no time for us to go back to the hotel, our baggage was packed and brought to the airport. Thus, covered with the Gobi Desert dust and telling effects of protecting ourselves from the cold, we must have been a sight and looked as terrible as we felt.

Subsequently, the Mongolian government invited me to come during the winter. Knowing that temperatures plunge down to -40°C, I did not want to repeat the experience of the earlier trip, so I requested them to schedule my visit to sometime after the winter months. They suggested spring which seemed fine to me, so I visited Ulaanbaatar during spring, only to discover that the temperature is usually around -25°C and seasonal blizzards are very common. Notwithstanding these untoward experiences, Mongolia is a fascinating country with pristine beauty, and I was fortunate to visit it several times and to witness the change taking place. During these visits, I also had the privilege to meet Kushok Bakula, a highly revered Buddhist Lama, who was India's Ambassador to Mongolia. He had tremendous goodwill and was highly respected as a supreme patriarch by both the top political leadership and all other diplomats in Mongolia.

I was to lead an ESCAP team to Pakistan in connection with a project to promote public-private partnership for sustainable development. Pakistan had been selected for developing a biodiversity park. All the members of the team received their visas except for me. There was barely a week left before the visit and I had still not received my laissez-passer with the visa. I assumed the hesitation was because of my Indian nationality. I called up the Pakistan Ambassador, whom I knew quite well and with whom I had played golf a few times, and told him frankly that I suspected that my nationality, notwithstanding my status as a UN staff member, was causing the problem and we may, therefore, be compelled to call off the visit of the UN team if there was any further delay in issuing a visa to me. He was very apologetic and after getting immediate clearance from Islamabad, got the visa issued promptly. To erase any misgiving on my part, the Ambassador got the government to organize a visit to my birth place, Abbottabad.

After the official commitments in Islamabad, a day's trip was organized to Abbottabad, just a couple of hours drive from Islamabad, escorted by a jeep load of policemen. Having left Abbottabad before the Partition as a child, I had no memories of the cantonment city except what my parents had told me. I nostalgically viewed the beautifully scenic surroundings of the now overcrowded city, especially the magnificent backdrop of mountains and the perennial rivulets flowing therefrom. These were known as *kathas* in the old days and public baths were built along them. I was unable to locate our family house which my father had told me was very close to the golf course. However, in the adjoining twin city, Nawansher, the *sawhneyian di gali* (the lane of the Sawhney's) still existed as did cement name slabs at the entrance of some houses representing the Sawhney families that had lived there. Word had spread that a Sawhney had come and there was a large crowd of local residents who followed me around. The more elderly were eager to talk to me and revive old memories. One of my family elders was the Honorary Magistrate there before the Partition and I visited his residence, still very regal with the Mughal garden adjoining it. It was then occupied by the police chief. I also visited what was originally a gurdwara, where my *namkaran* (naming ceremony) was done. It had now become a typical crowded local government office.

I was keen to buy something from my birthplace as a souvenir and my escorts suggested Peshawari *chappals* for which Abbottabad is famous. They took me to a shop where the then Prime Minister Nawaz Sharif bought his *chappals*. I selected a pair but the shopkeeper refused to take money from me. I eventually convinced him that I wanted to take something not only as a souvenir but to have the satisfaction of having spent some money at my birthplace. I also brought back a stone I picked up from a road near the golf course for sentimental reasons. When I showed it to Madhu, she thought I was being over-sentimental. I said to her that as she was born in Manhattan, New York, she wouldn't understand my nostalgia and sentiments.

Technical assistance to developing countries on trade policy formulation and capacity building for multilateral trade negotiations in General Agreement on Tariffs and Trade (GATT) and subsequently

World Trade Organization (WTO) was a priority area of our work. The Division undertook analysis of issues slated for global negotiations and their implications for developing countries. Unlike developed countries and the more advanced developing countries like India, most developing countries lacked the human and institutional capacity for effective participation in trade negotiations. Hence, the analytical work done by us was acknowledged as having provided very useful input for preparation of their national briefs. Our counterpart regional commissions—the Economic Commission for Africa and the Economic and Social Commission for West Asia—found our analysis very useful for their member countries as well. I was, therefore, invited as a resource person by both Commissions to participate in their preparatory meetings for global trade negotiations.

An unexpected situation requiring more than our normal kind of technical assistance was related to the issue of the Generalised System of Preferences (GSP), under which developed countries grant preferential tariffs on specific products to developing countries. The US was going to review its GSP regime, raising fears that some developing countries, particularly in the Asian region, might be totally graduated out or lose GSP privileges on specific products. A Senate Sub-Committee was to consider representations from developing countries. Surprisingly, none of the developing countries, potentially under threat, was prepared to make a representation to the Senate Committee. Therefore, we decided to make a general representation on behalf of all developing countries concerned in the region. I appeared before the Senate Sub- Committee in Washington and we were able to stall the action to graduate countries/products out of the GSP regime.

This visit to the USA was part of a crazy itinerary, combining a number of missions in three different continents in less than a week. I was in Fiji on a technical assistance mission from where I proceeded to Washington DC and thereon after two days to Berlin, Germany, where we held a leather goods export promotion exhibition and back to Bangkok after two days.

Along with trade policy matters, trade promotion activities involving the private sector also formed an important part of our programme, as many developing countries lacked the institutional capacity to undertake effective trade promotion. Product-specific studies were conducted on the potential for exports and imports for selected countries, with particular focus on the expansion of intra-regional trade as the rate of growth in intra-regional trade was outstripping growth elsewhere in the world. Organizing regional trade fairs became an important activity under this programme. Asia-Pacific International Trade Fairs (ASPAT) were organized in developing countries—Beijing (ASPAT 1994), Manila (ASPAT 1996), Almaty (ASPAT 1998), Seoul (ASPAT 1999) and Delhi (ASPAT 2000). The importance accorded to hosting these trade fairs could be gauged from the Philippines bringing out a postage stamp commemorating ASPAT 1996 and President Fidel Ramos hosting a dinner for all participants. On that occasion, during my discussions with President Ramos, I mentioned that apart from the focus on intra-regional trade, I was also exploring developing inter-regional trade linkages with South American countries, having already got a very positive response in my preliminary discussions with the Ambassadors of Argentina and Peru in Bangkok. He welcomed the initiative, saying that the Philippines, with its Spanish heritage, could be the gateway for Asia. In Delhi, ASPAT 2000 was integrated into the annual India International Trade Fair and Omar Abdullah, Union Minister of State, Commerce and Industry, and I jointly inaugurated the ASPAT fair.

In addition to ASPAT, we organized two specialized fairs in developed countries—a leather goods fair in Berlin, under a project funded by their government, and a handicrafts fair in Tokyo, Japan. I recall a remarkable incident in Berlin. At a buffet-style dinner reception hosted by the German government, an elderly gentleman came across to the table I was sitting with some of the participants and very politely asked if he could join us. I offered him the chair next to me and I introduced myself and he did likewise. At first, the name was not very audible but what I did hear very clearly was 'President of Germany'! I was startled by the informality and the absence of hangers-on and security personnel that one is used to seeing in most Asian countries. I was also uncertain whether I had heard him correctly but also didn't want to commit the indiscretion of seeking clarification. We got engaged in a casual conversation in the course of which I asked him whether he had visited India. He replied much to my relief that he had undertaken a 'State visit' a few years ago. He was Richard von Weizsäcker belonging to German nobility and now President. His unassuming manner and quiet elegance was admirable and I could not help but contrast him to the political leaders in India and how they would have reacted unattended and not fussed upon.

The Japanese government accepted my proposal to finance a project to promote the export of handicrafts from least developed countries as, in our assessment, beyond handicrafts, these countries had little to offer to the Japanese market, whereas handicrafts had potential for export, given the Japanese penchant for unique and inexpensive gift items. Prior to the event, a Japanese specialist in the marketing of handicrafts visited each of the participating countries to advise handicraft manufacturers on product development and packaging for the Japanese market. The fair proved to be very useful for a number of handicraft manufacturers from least developed countries to gain entry into the highly selective Japanese market.

In the midst of all this, the two-year extension on my secondment was ending and communications restarted from the Government of India. The tone of these was even blunter and compelled me to give serious consideration to either taking voluntary retirement or to return to India and rejoin the Punjab government. I had during an earlier visit to Chandigarh asked Kutty Nair, the then Chief Secretary, Punjab what would be the Punjab government's stand if I wanted to continue in the UN. His candid response was that there were so many secretary level officers in the Punjab secretariat, partly because most were reluctant to leave the comfort of being in Chandigarh to go on deputation to the Central government and some had not been considered suitable for empanelment by the Government of India for senior positions at the Centre. But, he said, when it came to allocating some important charge, it was difficult to find a suitable officer. He, therefore, summed up that if I decided to return, I would be welcome and could even select a particular post but in a converse situation, the Punjab government would have no problem in giving cadre clearance. As I learnt later, when the matter of my continuing in the UN was referred by the Central government to the Punjab government for cadre clearance, it was declined. There was then a new incumbent as Chief Secretary. The Central government was, therefore, insistent that I should return or resign.

A number of factors, both personal and professional, needed consideration before I could take a decision to continue in the UN or return to the Indian government. At the personal level, the family was happily settled in Bangkok. My two elder children were in senior school, studying for the International Baccalaureate diploma and to shift them back to the Indian educational system would have been unfair and disruptive. Continuing in the UN also gave me the option to send my children to any university in the world with financial support from the UN, something that would not be available to me back in India. These were very compelling considerations. After completing their schooling, Ravina went to a university in the USA and Aushima went to Australia.

At the professional level, I was enjoying my work and my involvement in dealing with important international developments. Apart from my direct charge as Director of the International Trade and Industry Division (in a restructuring of the secretariat, the Industry and Technology Division was merged into the Trade Division), I was managing and coordinating several important ESCAP initiatives and enjoyed a dominant position among my peers in the secretariat. Being in the UN was also a fulfilment of my original aspiration to join the diplomatic service and be involved in international diplomacy. And very importantly, the Executive Secretary was fully supportive of my continuing in the secretariat. I, therefore, took the decision to seek voluntary retirement from the IAS in 1997, after almost 30 years in government service. As I came to learn later, one of my IAS colleagues who was at the level of Secretary to Government, was very keen to replace me in ESCAP and was, thus, actively pushing the government's action to recall me, ignoring of course what Rafi had said earlier about the slim chances of an Indian national replacing me. Ironically, there was subsequently a change in the government policy which allowed officers, having put in the stipulated minimum years of service, the option to continue on secondment with international organisations indefinitely.

BIMSTEC

The multilateral trade negotiations in the WTO were protracted and becoming increasingly complex as the developed countries forcefully pushed their agenda. This created a strong divide between the developed countries and the developing countries. The Group of 77 (G77) at the UN, representing 134 developing countries, was itself seriously divided and lacked the cohesiveness to effectively counter the developed countries agenda. There was, therefore, a global trend for developing countries to simultaneously explore new areas of trade and economic cooperation among themselves.

In the early 1990s, ESCAP adopted a thematic work programme with regional economic cooperation as one of the three major themes. The Asia-Pacific region had been registering a dynamic rate of growth in intra-regional trade outstripping global averages on a sustained basis. There was a general recognition of the vast potential for further expansion of intra-regional trade and strengthening intraregional economic cooperation and integration.

Hence, under the thematic regional economic cooperation sub-programme adopted by ESCAP, special focus was given, inter alia, to strengthen institutional linkages among the existing subregional organisations, viz., ASEAN, SAARC, ECO and the Pacific Forum. ESCAP convened annual meetings with the heads of subregional organisations in an effort to build bridges for inter-subregional cooperation in selected areas with major emphasis on trade linkages. However, ESCAP's initial efforts in developing institutional linkages among the subregional organisations, particularly between ASEAN and SAARC, had not fructified. The acrimonious and tension-ridden relations between two of SAARC's major member countries, India and

Pakistan, made ASEAN reticent in developing institutional linkages for cooperation with SAARC. At the same time, some South Asian countries, in particular India, had adopted a 'Look East' policy to diversify their economic relations. Similarly, there was growing interest among some ASEAN countries to develop stronger trade relations with South Asian countries. In that prevailing situation, I visualised that an institutional mechanism for cooperation among the littoral states of the Bay of Bengal—linking some SAARC countries with some ASEAN countries—could have great potential and, therefore, acceptance among these countries. And very importantly, it would not include Pakistan.

I approached all the littoral states, including Myanmar, Thailand, Malaysia and Indonesia from ASEAN as well as Bangladesh, India and Sri Lanka from SAARC, through a letter explaining my proposal for establishing the Bay of Bengal economic community. The first response was from Malaysia with a positive interest in the proposed arrangement. Soon thereafter, Kobsak Chutikul, Director General, Foreign Ministry of Thailand, contacted me evincing interest in the proposal. He indicated that Thailand had recently adopted a 'Look West' policy and was visualizing the establishment of a growth triangle with India, given the large size of its economy and potentially a large market for Thailand's exports, and Sri Lanka because of the existing strong Buddhism-related linkages. He suggested we dovetail the two initiatives with the Thailand initiative as the first phase. We agreed to start the process with these three countries as Sri Lanka too was positively inclined. India having adopted a 'Look East' policy was also supportive of the initiative. In due course, Sheikh Hasina, Prime Minister of Bangladesh, became aware of this initiative and she approached her Indian counterpart, Atal Bihari Vajpayee, expressing her country's interest to be included in the new initiative.

An institutional arrangement was accordingly conceptualised for economic cooperation among the four countries within the ESCAP secretariat. We called the arrangement BISTEC (Bangladesh, India, Sri Lanka and Thailand Economic Cooperation), keeping in view Sri Lanka's reservation about the proposed name, Bay of Bengal Economic Community, as it did not consider itself to be located in the Bay of Bengal. We formulated a framework agreement along with the cooperative work programme, which at a ministerial meeting hosted by Thailand culminated in the Bangkok Declaration, creating BISTEC in June 1997. Myanmar, which initially participated as an observer, became a member at a ministerial meeting in Bangkok and the name changed to BIMSTEC.

The cooperative work programme had a major focus on trade, investment, multi-modal transport and communications. Connectivity by road and sea was considered crucial for deeper economic integration among the member countries. It was visualized that the strategic geographical location of the Andaman and Nicobar Islands could potentially make them a very important hub for developing coastal shipping, thereby increasing the number of seaports that are able to handle small- and medium-sized cargo vessels.

ESCAP functioned as the BIMSTEC secretariat for the initial years. A committee of the member countries based in Bangkok and a senior representative of the Thai Foreign Ministry met on a regular basis to advance the initiative. Chairmanship of the committee was held by rotation on a yearly basis. It was unfortunate that the then Indian Ambassador showed scant interest in the initiative even as Chairman, much to the disappointment of other Ambassadors. Gradually, management of the incipient organisation and its operations passed on to the member countries with the establishment of the secretariat in

Dhaka, Bangladesh. Subsequently, while the acronym BIMSTEC was retained, the name changed to the 'Bay of Bengal Initiative for Multi-Sectoral Technical and Economic Cooperation'. It now has seven countries as its members with the induction of Nepal and Bhutan on the basis of their access to the sea being through the Bay of Bengal.

As the one who initiated and conceptualised BIMSTEC, I have witnessed its progress with reservations in regard to both its membership and agenda. In my view, the membership is too limited on the ASEAN side and the agenda is too diverse and unwieldy. The membership is heavily skewed towards the SAARC countries as currently only two ASEAN countries, Myanmar and Thailand, are members. Malaysia was the first to respond to my proposal and should have been inducted in as a member. Indonesia and Singapore could be potential members. Lao PDR, which also has access to the sea through Thailand, should also be inducted on the same basis as Bhutan and Nepal. With the expanded membership and with a more balanced representation from both subregions, I am confident that BIMSTEC could realise its full potential as a framework agreement for deeper economic integration among the member countries and in translating the respective 'Look East' and 'Look West' policies to fruition. The work programme has become too dispersed and too rapidly. It needs to be more focused at this stage to giving priority to establishing a free trade area and strengthening physical connectivity through an all-weather road from Thailand to India as well as by developing coastal shipping.

I believe India, as a dominant country in BIMSTEC, could have played a more positive and proactive role instead of the ambivalence it has displayed, which, if one were to rationalise, is perhaps due to the existing skewed membership. The current membership is largely of South Asian countries, with which India already has bilateral trade arrangements. With Thailand, India has been involved in protracted negotiations on establishing a free trade area, which still remains inconclusive. The initial enthusiasm shown by India in BIMSTEC seemed to have waned after the first few years, perhaps being distracted by the initiation of another regional arrangement, the Regional Comprehensive Economic Partnership (RCEP) in the drafting of which India was actively involved. RCEP is essentially a free trade agreement and a larger grouping including important trading countries like China, Japan, Republic of Korea and Australia as well as several ASEAN countries. It was difficult to understand this ambivalence when the Government of India had already declared a 'Look East' policy but apparently with no serious intent to implement it within the framework of BIMSTEC. Moreover, quite clearly, the SAARC process was virtually stymied by the irreconcilable political differences between India and Pakistan and hence, it is not going achieve anything meaningful.

I felt that India could leverage this arrangement strategically to consolidate economic cooperation and integration among the littoral states of the Bay of Bengal and thereby check the spread of Chinese influence in this subregion. China's determination to spread its hegemony across the Asian countries, inter alia, through its Belt and Road Initiative (BRI) and under the RCEP, should have been compelling reasons for India to rethink its approach and policy towards BIMSTEC, imperatively as a strategy to counter China's designs to spread its influence in this region.

Soon after the BJP came into power in 2014, I met with Nripendra Misra, the then Principal Secretary to Prime Minister Narendra Modi and having previously interacted with him during his tenure in the Commerce Ministry. When I mentioned BIMSTEC to him, he appeared indifferent and alluded to RCEP as being of greater interest. I was nonplussed by this reaction as I felt that BIMSTEC offered a viable framework agreement for economic cooperation and integration in pursuance of the new government's 'Act East' and 'Neighbourhood First' declarations.

More recent events, however, signal a more positive intent in India's attitude to developing a more integrated partnership with BIMSTEC. In 2016 when India was BIMSTEC chairman, Prime Minister Narendra Modi hosted a retreat for BIMSTEC leaders and the BRICS-BIMSTEC Outreach Summit in Goa. Subsequently, when he reassumed the Prime Ministership, he invited all BIMSTEC leaders to attend his swearing-in function in New Delhi in 2019. India's withdrawal from RCEP after having been actively involved in its drafting, as it did not consider the final charter to be consistent with its national interests, could also have been a factor in its according greater importance and attention to BIMSTEC.

These overtures were indicative of India's more substantive involvement in BIMSTEC and not just for political optics as was borne out in the fifth summit held on 30 March 2022. Prime Minister Modi acknowledged in his statement that BIMSTEC was a bridge of connectivity, prosperity and security in the Bay of Bengal. He emphasized its importance as an architecture to strengthen economic integration and trade connectivity among the member countries. These were not mere rhetorical statements as the Prime Minister backed them up by announcing significant donations for both the strengthening of the secretariat in Dhaka and the work programme. This summit, therefore, could be a watershed in India playing a more active leadership role in shaping BIMSTEC's future development and in the implementation of the Charter adopted at a summit commemorating 25 years of its existence.

In the ESCAP secretariat, there was a change again in the post of Executive Secretary. Mooy, having completed his five-year tenure, was succeeded by Kim Hak-Su from South Korea. There was a striking difference in their style of functioning. Mooy had years earlier worked in the ESCAP secretariat and had a more affable, or what one might say, ASEAN style of functioning. Kim Hak-Su came determined to make an immediate impact as a strong and decisive leader, at times openly showing little regard for his predecessor, and so in contrast could appear to be overbearing. Shortly after Kim Hak-Su took charge as Executive Secretary, he decided to reshuffle some of the Directors, and as one learnt later, this was with an ulterior motive. I was shifted to the Environment and Sustainable Development Division to replace a specialist in water resources, who was sent to the Social Development Division. The Director of the Population Division, an expert in demography, was shifted to replace me in the Trade Division. That reshuffle of senior staff was unprecedented and it sent shock waves across the secretariat. Both the affected Directors met the Executive Secretary and expressed their discontentment with his decision as they had no expertise related to their new assignments.

Kim Hak-Su called me to explain that he had decided to shift me not because of any dissatisfaction with my Division's work, but he actually wanted to shift the other two from their current charges and consequently, I was shifted. Moreover, he wanted me to take charge of the Environment and Sustainable Division because he had confidence that under my charge, the preparatory work would be undertaken properly for the forthcoming World Summit on Sustainable Development (WSSD) in Johannesburg, South Africa, which was due in less than two years. I responded that I would have preferred to continue in my current post, having put in considerable effort in building up the Division. However, if that were to be his decision, I would have no problem in managing the new Division, having come with a career background of diversified experience. On the other hand, I expressed empathy for the other two Directors, who were reshuffled. I told him it was like putting square pegs in round holes.

Kim Hak-Su confided that he had deliberately shifted the other two to posts he was aware would make them unhappy, hoping that might push them to seek early retirement. I was taken aback by his devious thinking and the fact that he had not given any consideration to the potential damage he was doing to the functioning of the secretariat and its credibility. As I had expected, neither of them sought early retirement and we had two disgruntled heads of Divisions. Kim Hak-Su's lack of experience in working in an international organisation, and hence his occasional overbearing demeanour, was not helping the work environment in the secretariat. Personally, I received due regard from Kim Hak-Su and at our weekly senior staff meetings he would invariably go along with my views. His demeanour towards me remained free from the short shrift he gave to most of my peers.

On leaving the International Trade and Industry Division after having been its Director for over 12 years, my farewell message to my colleagues dated 23 January 2001 eloquently reflects my sentiments:

> Dear Colleagues,
>
> As I prepare to leave this Division on my transfer to ENRD, I reflect on the time I have spent here. I have been here for a little over 12 years—a period that has been eventful and very challenging in many ways, whether it was the

external environment of an unprecedented economic boom and thereafter an equally unprecedented financial crises in the region or internally, the reform process in the ESCAP secretariat.

The evolution of this Division has itself been an exciting and often challenging process, culminating in the merger of two Divisions into ITTD. From a rather modest sized Division with limited resources, human and financial, it has grown to a vibrant and dynamic unit with an impressive programme of work and, more importantly, record of performance. The Division is now poised to take on an even more significant role and greater responsibilities in the future. We should all feel proud and justifiably so, to have been a part of this dynamic process and to have contributed to it.

For me personally, this has been a very enriching and memorable experience. I, therefore, leave with a tremendous sense of satisfaction and fulfilment as well as a feeling of gratitude towards all my colleagues, professional and general service staff, both past and present, for all the support and cooperation extended to me in the discharge of my functions. I look forward to my next assignment as an exciting new challenge and an opportunity to further enrich my knowledge and experience.

Dear colleagues, our happy association transcends the boundaries of time and secretariat structures. I am, therefore, not saying farewell as I am sure we will meet again, whether in meeting rooms or corridors and other common places

> here in the secretariat or outside. I would, however, like to extend to each one of you my best wishes for your success in future. May you and your family enjoy the best of health and every happiness always.

The Environment and Sustainable Development Division had three sections dealing with environment policy, water resources and energy related issues, with specialists as Section Chiefs. My predecessor, having been a specialist in water resources, was most comfortable concentrating on the work of that section, leaving the other two sections to work more or less independently. Consequently, there was some initial resistance, particularly in the environment section, to my overseeing its work but soon it was realised that I was a more hands-on manager and was trying to make the sections work in a more cohesive and integrated manner. To assist developing countries in their preparatory work for WSSD was our priority. It involved preparation of substantive documents and organizing a series of inter-governmental meetings to discuss issues slated to come up in WSSD. The Executive Secretary and I attended the summit on behalf of ESCAP.

Johannesburg, the venue of WSSD, is reputedly an unsafe city with lurking danger of being mugged or assaulted. The entire venue, where the summit was held, and the adjoining hotels were barricaded so that local people could not enter without authorisation. The delegations had been advised to stay in hotels located within the barricaded premises. The Swiss delegation, for some inexplicable reason, decided to stay in a hotel outside the protected area and, on the very first day, had a break-in, reportedly losing their computers. The summit culminated in the adoption of The Johannesburg Declaration on Sustainable Development which was built on the decisions taken by previous conferences with greater emphasis on multilateralism in addressing critical environment related issues. Following the summit, substantive work in ESCAP focused on the Plan of Implementation of WSSD adopted at the summit. However, soon after the summit, Kim Hak-Su asked me to move to the office of the Executive Secretary as his Principal Officer. As Principal Officer, SPECA remained my main responsibility and so I was able to devote more time to the development of this programme in Central Asia. In addition, I dealt with issues requiring inter-divisional coordination, with a special focus on vulnerable countries, namely Myanmar, North Korea and Timor Leste.

I remained as Principal Officer till my retirement in March 2004. However, Kim Hak-Su, supported by the Executive Secretary of UNECE, asked the UN Headquarters to extend my service, citing my indispensability for implementation of SPECA. We had an understanding with UNECE that we would alternately take the role of chief coordinator on an annual basis and it was now ESCAP's turn to take on the responsibility. Hence, my continuance in service was felt indispensable. Granting extension in service was not going to be easy as at that time, the UN policy was against extension of service post retirement and rehiring of retirees. However, with the two Executive Secretaries seeking my extension, an exception was made in my case.

I continued, in the interim, on a consultancy contract as Senior Advisor to the Executive Secretary, and after the approval was received, I resumed my responsibility as Principal Officer, extending over a period of another two years. During that period, I had to travel frequently to the Central Asian countries to advance the SPECA initiative. Turkmenistan and Uzbekistan continued to be reticent in their participation, whereas Azerbaijan, which geographically is not a part of Central Asia, evinced keen interest and later became a member.

Afghanistan, which has common stakes with some of the Central Asian countries, particularly relating to water resources management, also became a member, thus enlarging SPECA's membership to seven countries.

The intergovernmental structure for the implementation of SPECA was also strengthened. The Regional Advisory Committee, consisting of senior officials from member states and coordinators of the two regional commissions, was established which met frequently to develop the work programme and impart momentum to the implementation of the programme. Project Working Groups were established in the areas of transport and cross-border facilitation, led by Kazakhstan; rational and effective use of energy and water resources, led by Kyrgyzstan; and organizing an international economic conference, led by Tajikistan. In addition, two Working Groups—one on trade and trade facilitation, which was of particular significance for the landlocked and doubly landlocked countries, and second on statistics—were established. In 2006 the Governing Council, the apex body represented at the ministerial level, was constituted and its first session was hosted by Azerbaijan in Baku.

I introduced the institution of an Economic Forum to be attended by policymakers, specialists, private sector and other UN agencies and international organisations, which was to meet just prior to the Governing Council meeting. It was intended to provide a forum for experts to deliberate on important issues and report to the policy making apex body. The first meeting of the Economic Forum was organized in Baku, immediately preceding the Governing Council meeting. That was a time when oil exporting countries were gaining windfall profits, which among the SPECA states included Azerbaijan, Kazakhstan, Turkmenistan, and to some extent, Uzbekistan. The agenda for the inaugural Economic Forum was, therefore, focused on the energy dividend and how the growth impulse in the oil exporting countries could be spread for prosperity and stability across the SPECA region. The hypothesis presented was that within the SPECA region, there could not be islands of prosperity surrounded by impoverished countries. To make development in the region more sustainable, it was imperative to spread the growth impulse across the region through deeper economic cooperation and integration.

A looming crisis in Central Asia was the rapid shrinking of the Aral Sea, one of the largest man-made lakes in the world, located between Kazakhstan and Uzbekistan but serving the entire region. The uncontrolled withdrawal of water from the Aral Sea was leading to an environmental catastrophe in the region. The Presidents of the Central Asian countries took the initiative to establish the International Fund for Saving the Aral Sea (IFAS) to improve the ecological and socio-economic situation in the basin of the Aral Sea. In ESCAP, we were exploring how the UN system could assist IFAS. In that process, I met the head of IFAS in Tashkent, who was formerly a Deputy Minister in the Soviet government. We met in his office and to save time, he organized the typical *kabab* lunch and local beer in the office. Over lunch, he suddenly diverted to talking about Raj Kapoor and the song 'Awara hoon' which had become famous across the entire Soviet Union. As he hummed the song, I joined in with a few lines I could remember and then I saw this huge bald man with tears rolling down his cheeks, hugging me and telling me how much he loved the movie *Awara*. I met several such men in Central Asia occupying high positions, who either suffered similar nostalgia, perhaps not so emotionally, about the movie *Awara* or having spent a memorable part of their lives spent in India.

At the time of my final retirement, SPECA had been firmly established which was a matter of some satisfaction, considering the newly independent states were going through a process of transition to a market economy, a process that was unguided by any historical precedent. Old institutions, linked to the socialist system, had been dismantled and till new institutions were established, there was a kind of vacuum. Perhaps even more difficult was changing the mindset of the government officials, after having worked in a totally different work environment before gaining independence. Hence, when I retired from ESCAP July-end 2006, I felt I was leaving on a high note and I could look back to my career in the United Nations with a great deal of fulfilment and satisfaction and having left a lasting legacy, most significantly, of adding to the regional architecture of inter-governmental institutions, the institutions of BIMSTEC and SPECA. These institutions are now well established arrangements for regional economic cooperation and periodic Summits are attended by Heads of Governments. And for Thailand, which had been my home country for almost two decades, a premier educational institution, NIST.

11

Post-Retirement: Anti-Climax

In three words I can sum up everything
I've learned about life: it goes on.

—Robert Frost

At the turn of the millennium, the United Nations hosted at its headquarters in New York, the World Peace Summit organized by the World Peace Foundation. The Secretary-General of the Foundation was Bawa Jain, a very close friend of ours. Eminent religious leaders representing all major religions from across the world attended the summit and agreed to constitute the World Council of Religious Leaders (WCRL). They interacted on how they could contribute to achieving a more peaceful and environmentally sustainable world, acknowledging that religion was the underpinning in many conflicts. As a follow-up to this milestone conference, the World Millennium

Peace Foundation (WMPF) was established in Bangkok with the aim, inter alia, to promote youth leadership.

Madhu was asked by Bawa Jain to run the Foundation and she, known for her missionary zeal, immediately got extremely busy in organizing the first World Youth Peace Summit. It was held in Bangkok attended by an unexpected large number of aspiring youth leaders from across the world. The Foundation also initiated and implemented projects to assist children's education ('each one teach one') and to provide alternative sources of income to impoverished women, living in the Thailand-Lao PDR border area. Hence, it was a time when both Madhu and I were very busy in our respective occupations. In fact, Ravina had completed her undergrad studies in Seattle and was very enthusiastically involved with Madhu in youth-related projects. Aushima was in Sydney doing her undergrad course in mass communication and acting. Raisa had joined NIST and had quite independently settled in well without close parental supervision. In fact, she organized her school life so well that we never had to worry about her being an achiever.

After retirement I had also got more involved in the WMPF. While still in ESCAP, I had participated as a resource person in a conference on sustainable development, organized jointly with the UN in Bangkok. After the successful Youth Summit, the King of Jordan indicated interest in hosting a similar conference in Amman. Bawa Jain and I visited Amman and met the King's adviser and other senior officials in his secretariat. Matters seemed to be progressing well when the untoward happened. One night, there were simultaneous bomb blasts in several American-owned hotels in Amman. Fortunately, the hotel we were staying in, though also American owned, was spared. It, however, created a security threat which could not be ignored and plans to hold the conference there had to be deferred. Eminent Buddhist Masters in Taiwan were also very active in following up on the WCRL Summit, and Madhu and I participated in their conferences in Taipei.

Soon after retirement, offers started coming from my erstwhile colleagues in ESCAP to undertake consultancy assignments. Though that was easy picking, I politely declined as I did not want to have to report to those who I had either recruited or in whose career development I had been involved. I had done one consultancy assignment and that was as Senior Advisor to the Executive Secretary and so that remained my threshold. I did, however, undertake consultancy assignments for other UN agencies, of which two were very interesting, albeit for entirely different reasons.

One assignment was for the United Nations Office for Project Services (UNOPS) relating to North Korea. The Government of Japan and UK's Department for International Development (DFID) had jointly funded a remote sensing project in North Korea, inter alia, to study the pattern of water resources and sea waves in the context of recent famines there. After the completion of the first five-year phase, the project was up for consideration by the two donors for its extension into the second phase. However, there was evidence-based fear that the equipment supplied for remote sensing was allegedly being used by North Korean agencies for other surveillance purposes as well, threatening the security of neighbouring countries, namely South Korea and Japan. As the project was under consideration for its second phase, the donor countries wanted the equipment requirement submitted by North Korea reviewed and curtailed, especially equipment that could be used for dual purposes, before extending any further financial assistance.

I led a small team to North Korea to undertake a review of project implementation in the first phase and to recommend its future parameters and equipment requirement for the next phase, keeping in view of course the security concerns of the neighbouring countries. In Pyongyang, we were assisted by the country UNDP office. In all my previous missions to North Korea, I had never been accorded the kind of hospitality that was extended to the team during that visit. It included an overnight stay at a *dacha* where spring water at 42 degrees Centigrade temperature flowed into the bathtub as well as an evening at a karaoke lounge, which was not accessible to anyone but VIP foreign visitors, duly escorted by local hosts. I believe we were able to complete that assignment to the satisfaction of the two donor countries.

The other consultancy assignment was on behalf of the International Fund for Agriculture Development (IFAD) to review implementation of a project related to food security in the North-Eastern states of India. It was essentially a micro-finance project with an innovative methodology. The target group were landless women who eked out an existence by doing daily labour—a seasonal occupation which gave them just about three months food security. These women were formed into self-help groups (SHGs) where they were trained for self-management. Each SHG was allotted a corpus of funds which it managed and provided micro-finance to its members for supplementary occupation like poultry farming, kitchen gardens, etc. The project succeeded in increasing food security from the earlier three months to about nine months a year. It was also encouraging to note that there were no cases of default in any of the SHGs. And a positive spin-off was that the beneficiary women became more conscious of improving their lives, particularly through better hygiene and education for their children. The project also provided funds to encourage the menfolk to get involved in developing local infrastructure. The review report was sent to the National Planning Commission with the recommendation to continue the project with more intensive coverage in the North-Eastern states.

In January 2007, Ban Ki-moon, former Foreign Minister of South Korea, became the Secretary-General of the UN. It was expected that Kim Hak-Su, who was due to complete his five-year tenure as Executive Secretary of ESCAP, would get an extension but quite surprisingly that did not happen. The new Secretary-General was reportedly determined to make changes wherever senior level posts were falling vacant. It seemed a very opportune time for India to make a bid for the post of Executive Secretary, ESCAP. The first two Executive Secretaries of ESCAP had been Indians but after that it had been more than 50 years and no Indian had occupied that post which informally went by a kind of rotation, mostly between the ASEAN and South Asian countries. Kim Hak-Su of South Korea was an exception.

I started receiving some encouraging signals from former colleagues in the UN system, particularly in the headquarters, to contest for the post, keeping in view my experience and reputation in the Asia-Pacific region. To my surprise, the Indian Government was not contemplating putting up a candidate for the post. I met the then Foreign Secretary Shyam Saran and subsequently his successor Shiv Shankar Menon as well as Principal Secretary to Prime Minister, Kutty Nair, whom I had known from my earliest days in the IAS in Hoshiarpur, where he was Deputy Commissioner. Eventually, after considerable effort on my part, the government nominated me as its candidate. However, soon thereafter, I began to realise that the government, though having nominated me, was not really pushing my candidature. Having easier access to Kutty Nair, I met him more frequently to express my concerns about the apparently half-hearted support I was receiving from the government. Each time he would assure me that he would speak to the Foreign Secretary but there appeared no tangible change in the government's attitude.

To further exacerbate matters, the Indian Ambassador to the UN and the Chef de Cabinet to the UN Secretary-General, who also happened to be an Indian, appeared to have total lack of rapport between them, and I often found myself being the medium of communication between the two. In great frustration, I approached Kutty Nair and Shiv Shankar Menon and pleaded that if it was felt that I was not the right candidate, then I was ready to be replaced but the government should at least show some commitment and seriousness in making its bid for the post. I had also been in contact with Pranab Mukherjee who was then Foreign Minister. He appeared very supportive and had even given me his mobile number to keep him informed, especially during weekends when he sometimes travelled to Kolkata. But all to no avail.

It was more through the efforts of my former colleagues in the UN headquarters that I was interviewed for the post, albeit through a tele-conference. Through the feedback I later received, my interview went off well and the interviewers were impressed with my knowledge of the region as well as my experience in ESCAP. However, from the grapevine it appeared that the Secretary-General, having failed to appoint a female as Executive Secretary of ESCWA in the face of resistance by Saudi Arabia, was under pressure to appoint a female in ESCAP. It was a Friday when I received a telephone call from Ambassador Kim, who was the Secretary-General's Deputy and as his close confidant, was on the interview board. He was with the

Secretary-General on a visit to Los Angeles. He said that he had called me to inform me in advance of a formal announcement in the following week that although I was considered to be on merit the most suitable candidate, the Secretary-General was under immense pressure to appoint a female. Hence, he was extending me the courtesy to inform me in advance why I had not been selected. He then asked me whether I would be willing to work with the new incumbent as her advisor. My immediate reaction was to express regret that merit had been overlooked and so I was not inclined to accept the offer to be an advisor to the new incumbent. Soon thereafter, I received a message from a well-wisher in the UN headquarters advising me that I should immediately get my government to intervene and insist on a merit-based selection. As an important country in the region, it would not be easy for the Secretary-General to ignore India's intervention. In a similar situation in the Middle East, the Secretary-General had bowed down to the Saudi Arabian protest to ignore merit and select on gender basis.

I immediately informed both Kutty Nair and Shiv Shankar Menon by email and met them to request the government's immediate intervention. I suggested that the Foreign Ministry immediately convey to the Secretary-General to withhold any announcement till the matter had been discussed with the Indian Government. Shiv Shankar Menon assured me a call by the Foreign Minister would be made the following Monday. As the Foreign Minister was leaving for the Philippines over the weekend, his Special Assistant was expected to be instructed to make the call from there. On Monday I was not getting any confirmation from the Foreign Ministry, so I called Manila to contact the Foreign Minister's staff. To my utter disappointment, the Special Assistant said that he was totally unaware of the matter as no such instructions had been given to him!

The formal announcement of the appointment of the new Executive Secretary came within two days. I was perplexed over the abysmal manner in which the matter had been handled, in fact right from inception, by the officials concerned at the highest level and their lack of serious intent and commitment to uphold national interest. It was very difficult to understand that the government having declared a 'Look East' policy, the Foreign Ministry was so lackadaisical when there was an opportunity to have an Indian heading the principal UN agency in the region. I did have one final meeting with Kutty Nair in his office and gave vent to my frustration and disappointment over how the entire matter had been handled from the very beginning. This was by far the most regretful and disappointing turn of events in my career. For me personally, it was a betrayal of trust but it also smacked of a gross lack of accountability at the senior most levels of bureaucracy. As one not to give up, when the opportunity came again five years later, I tried to meet the new Foreign Secretary, Sujata Singh. She had earlier been posted in the Embassy in Bangkok and was dealing with ESCAP. Hence, we met quite often and she confided in me whenever she needed advice. I, therefore, felt confident in approaching her. Much to my disillusionment, she always seemed to be too preoccupied to even give me an appointment. India lost again by default and the new Executive Secretary, though from South Asia, was a lady from Pakistan.

I have tried to understand this behavioural pattern which seems unique to Indian bureaucracy in not exerting wholehearted effort in seizing an opportunity in the country's interest. In spite of having been in the system, this mindset has baffled and disappointed me. In a striking contrast, when the post of Secretary-General of the Commonwealth Secretariat fell vacant, the entire might of the Government, particularly the Foreign Ministry, was put into action, even though the relevance of that organisation in the current context to India's interests was questionable. It could only be attributed to the exercise of an extra-constitutional political patronage.

Notwithstanding my unsuccessful bid for the top UN post in the region, Madhu and I decided to continue to live in Bangkok. Having spent so many uninterrupted years there, in contrast to the inevitable transfers in a government job, it had virtually become a second home. Moreover, for our children it seemed to be their preferred place to live. This became even more definite when our eldest daughter Ravina decided to marry Dhruv, an old school friend, whose family is settled in Bangkok. Dhruv too was professionally based in Bangkok, so this is where Ravina would live after marriage. They were married in November 2007 in Delhi, a memorable week of functions that blended Indian traditions with the more modern styles of celebration.

Post-retirement, life became quieter and more relaxed. There were a few soundings to work in the private sector but I was not interested to work for any one and thereby compromise my independence. I preferred to remain an independent international consultant and be very selective in whatever assignment I would undertake. My thought process was that this was the stage in life when one should do what one wants to do and derives enjoyment from it, especially after a lifetime of mostly doing what one was told or had to do.

My involvement with NIST continued. I had been appointed Founding Member for life as a gesture of gratitude for my role in the establishment of the school. I was also more involved in Bawa Jain's initiatives following the Millennium Peace Summit. And then, golf became my favourite pastime, given the large number of amazing golf courses in Thailand together with the camaraderie that came with it.

Madhu was enjoying her work in the Millennium Peace Foundation and was kept busy. Aushima had completed her education in Sydney and had moved to Mumbai to fulfil a long cherished dream to act in Bollywood movies. Watching Raisa enjoying her schooling in a truly international environment in NIST was a very satisfying feeling and a vindication of what we had aspired for in establishing the School. She later joined the Australia National University in Canberra, with a group of her school friends and settled in very quickly.

As life goes on normally, inevitably the unexpected happens and disrupts everything. First, it was my overdoing in the golf driving range which resulted in a surgery for a torn rotator cuff. But soon thereafter, we faced the horrible tragedy of the untimely demise of Madhu's younger brother Sidharth. Having just returned from London to Mumbai and after a busy day in office, he decided to unwind playing squash and tragically collapsed there. This heart-wrenching tragedy was further exacerbated by the revival of memories of her elder brother Kavi, having prematurely passed away years before. Sidi, as he was affectionately called, had become so much a part of my father-in-law's daily life that the loss was unbearable for him. His health began to slide and his zest for life was also gradually but visibly fading away.

While we continued to live in Bangkok, Madhu had to spend more time in India taking care of her mother and father. We encouraged them to visit us in Bangkok which was always a good change for them. It also revived their years-old association and friendship, especially with the King and Queen of Thailand, with whom they had enjoyed a special relationship when my father-in-law was Ambassador to Thailand. At short notice, His Majesty would meet with my father-in-law either in Bangkok or Hua Hin and they would spend hours together.

Similarly, whenever my mother-in-law visited Bangkok, she would have an audience with Her Majesty. On one visit, Her Majesty invited us to dinner at the Grand Palace. It was a most memorable experience spending that evening with Her Majesty, in a setting bereft of excessive protocol. Her Majesty personally took us around the Grand Palace to show the artefacts she had selected for placement there. The conversation over dinner was light-hearted extending also to the selection of music the Naval Band was playing which, as Her Majesty informed, included some of His Majesty's favourites when he was courting Her Majesty.

On 23 June 2010, Ravina gave birth to Riana, and Madhu and I celebrated the joy of becoming grandparents. Aushima, having done a few movies in Bollywood, returned to Bangkok. She was ready to get married to Sanjeev Saluja (Sanj), her friend for many years, when both were studying in Bangkok and Sydney. Sanj and his family are also settled in Bangkok, so Aushima, like Ravina, was going to continue to be living in Bangkok. This was perfect, having all our children living in the same city. We agreed to have the wedding in Thailand. Ravina, along with her two friends Sharan and Ruchika, had set up a wedding planning company called 'Pink Palki' and they took on all the arrangements for the wedding which was held in a resort hotel in Rayong. The wedding was attended by our close family and good old friends, and I felt, as also many others, it was one of the most fun weddings in an enchanting setting I had ever attended. At times it felt more like a carnival including a surprise performance by the famous Tiffany in Pattaya, dancing to Bollywood music. On 15 October 2015, Aushima gave birth to Aryan and we became proud grandparents for the second time of two adorable babies.

After the wedding, Madhu needed to spend more time with her father in Delhi because of his deteriorating health condition. What was earlier a chronic back pain turned out to be terminal cancer of the pancreas. It had been kept a secret from him but then eventually it had to be revealed to him. His passing away, preceded by Kavi and Sidi, left just Madhu and her mother, who was also keeping indifferent health, and preferred to live in Mumbai where medical attention was more assured and reliable. My father too had been in and out of hospital mainly due to age-related ailments. He wanted to live to be a centenarian and after having crossed the mid-nineties, he would often count the remaining years and tell me that I must help him to reach hundred. He had entered his hundredth year when he was admitted to hospital where he passed away peacefully.

The possibility of my returning to Punjab emerged when during a conversation with Madhu's cousin, Capt. Amarinder Singh (Yuvie), he accepted my offer to articulate his vision for Punjab and elaborate it with an implementation programme. We developed the vision and programme and it was to be an important basis for fighting the Assembly elections in 2012. Yuvie wanted my commitment to be his advisor if he came to power as Chief Minister for implementing the programme, which I readily accepted with the confidence that I understood both the situation in Punjab and the functioning of the bureaucracy there. Unfortunately, the Congress lost the election and our plan never came to fruition. However five years later, the Congress was back to power with Yuvie as Chief Minister. We had a brief discussion on reviving the vision-related programme but came to no conclusion. I did, however, note bemusedly in news telecasts some of the ministers carrying that document to meetings. As it transpired subsequently, serious infighting in the Congress resulted in Yuvie's exit not just from the chief ministership but also the party he had served with distinction for several decades. With the massive change in the political scenario following the recent elections, I do not visualise the current dispensation giving any attention to the vision document and, for that matter, any future effort on my part to resurrect it.

It was that stage in life when the passing of a senior family member or school friend made one feel vulnerable and more conscious of staying healthy. But then one also realises that there is no chronological order. My youngest brother Rajive had been diagnosed with multiple myeloma when he was at the peak of his profession as a senior advocate in the Supreme Court and a pillar of support to the whole family. After protracted treatment at King's College Hospital, London, stem cell transplant was considered imperative. Having a hundred per cent DNA match, I became his donor. We went to London, accompanied by Madhu and Minoo, to go through the procedure which was completed successfully. It was also an opportunity for us to spend some memorable time together, something we had not been able to do for ages. A few months later Rajive went back to London for the stem cell transplant but during a preliminary procedure involving a biopsy of his kidney, clumsiness caused his kidney to be irreparably damaged. Rajive could never recover from that in spite of further treatment in the USA and his health condition deteriorated rapidly. In his untimely and horribly tragic passing on, the loss to the family was irreparable, of one who was the youngest of us three brothers but in many ways stood the tallest.

12

Brief Reflections

Do not be desirous of having things done quickly.
Do not look at small advantages.
Desire to have done things quickly
prevents their being done thoroughly.
Looking at small advantages
prevents great affairs from being accomplished.

—Confucius

As I now reflect back on my life and career, it has certainly been both challenging and eventful. The progression from working at the sub-national to the national and then on to the international arena as well as the range and diversity of experiences that I went through, was nothing short of phenomenal. It was, in a sense, a '20-20' career, having spent 20 years in the national scene and then almost 20 years at the international level.

Living a life is all about making choices whenever confronted with challenges and opportunities and how one responds to them. I certainly had my share of them. The soft choices always looked more tempting as invariably it was the easier way out. The choices I made, whether in dealing with particular situations like what I confronted as District Magistrate when on more than one occasion I deviated from government directives or at different stages of my career itself, I did with a sense of conviction, and invariably ending with a sense of vindication and fulfilment. Yes, there were disappointments but it was easier to accept these, having exerted myself fully to do whatever I could within the limits of my control. In the natural progression of dealing with situations, having exerted oneself fully, a stage then comes when one has to leave it for things to happen in the normal course. If the expected happens well and good, if not, then it was not to be.

A fleeting glimpse of my career would indicate the full spectrum of my diverse experience—from working at the village level coaxing the poverty-stricken to take on supplementary occupation and accompanying them to cattle fairs to buy buffaloes, to sitting with Presidents of Central Asian countries advocating macroeconomic policy initiatives in their transition to market economies; from setting up village cooperative societies and a cooperative union milk plant, which now is benefitting thousands of the poorest rural families, to establishing inter-governmental institutional arrangements at the international level (BIMSTEC and SPECA) which now form a significant part of the Asia-Pacific regional architecture of international institutions for regional economic cooperation and integration; from fulfilling a debt to my alma mater as a member of the school board and to managing a crisis in a rural college to establishing an international school (NIST) which in a short span of time has become a premier educational institution in Thailand.

These are only some broad contours on the canvass on which the story of my life could be painted. A painting of my life might only be figurative but paintings and art have been a passion in my life. My parents were always house-proud and gardening was their passion. Madhu's family, too, has one of the finest collections of art and antiquities, which became an added inspiration for me. Even as a youngster, I would visit art shops or auctions and pick up a piece of art to take back home. Then there was the inspirational visit to the Salar Jung Museum in Hyderabad during the Bharat Darshan undertaken while training in the IAS.

My frequent travels, both while in government and at the UN, gave me immense opportunities to explore and collect art and objets d'art, some of considerable antiquity value, reflecting the culture of different countries and ranging from the traditionally religious 'Tanjore's', *Tankhas*, Buddha images, Russian orthodox icons to antique porcelain and silverware as well as traditional Korean cabinets (some with Kenji script), Persian and Central Asian carpets. What makes the eclectic collection even more special is that there are many interesting anecdotes relating to many of my collectibles. Hence, a viewing of my collection is like walking down memory lane. I hope one day I will document these anecdotes as well.

I consider myself to have been particularly fortunate to have had friendships I have enjoyed in my life. Bonds that were forged in school days and very early in my career remain at the core and I feel enriched by these associations. Like an elixir that makes me recapture the joyful days of our youth. As life goes on, one loses some friends, but their memories remain etched in one's heart. When I moved to Thailand, I was aware I would miss meeting my good old friends on a regular basis. But we have made new friends in Bangkok and, for me especially, there is the camaraderie I enjoy with my golfing friends.

I believe the greatest inspiration in my life initially came from my father. His own life story as an adopted child through a family settlement; his life as a child under threat from relatives of his adoptive father over his estate; consequently, his biological father giving up all claims on his behalf to secure his life, hence deprived of inheritance from both his biological and adoptive family as well as, excluded from any right to compensation after the Partition; providing shelter to several members of the extended family in the aftermath of the Partition; giving us the best upbringing and opportunity for education; and above all, he never ever talked about any of this leave alone complain. He was non-interfering in the lives of us three brothers believing that his children could do no wrong and yet at the most crucial crossroads of my life, his advice guided my future. And in all this, my mother stood steadfast with him, giving him the courage and strength when needed to take life-changing decisions. This upbringing made me a family man cherishing the values of a closely bonded family.

Madhu has been the perfect life partner and companion and someone I could turn to for support whenever facing conflicting choices. She is full of energy and action-oriented; always for 'do it now' whenever I was guilty of vacillating or procrastinating. We might have different likes and dislikes on matters which one might consider are somewhat trivial, like the preferred choice of movies and my life-long passion for sports.

Our three, absolutely adorable daughters Ravina, Aushima and Raisa—carefully and beautifully brought up by Madhu—are admirably ingrained with values and respect for Indian traditions and culture, in spite of living in a foreign country right from their formative years.

And of course, our two grandchildren. Riana, now 12 years of age, is as bright as a sparkling star and ever so multi-talented, be it gymnastics, stage performances in hip-hop dancing, ballet and singing. Aryan, who is 6, is already an amazing communicator and entertainer.

My family is indeed the greatest blessing God could have given me, and in living my life the way I did, they have been and are the abiding inspiration.

Index